The Home

PENELOPE MORTIMER

The Home

HUTCHINSON OF LONDON

HUTCHINSON & CO (*Publishers*) LTD
3 Fitzroy Square, London W1

London Melbourne Sydney Auckland
Wellington Johannesburg Cape Town
and agencies throughout the world

First published 1971

*This book has been set in Garamond type, printed in Great Britain
on antique wove paper by Anchor Press, and
bound by Wm. Brendon, both of Tiptree, Essex*

ISBN 0 09 108810 0

Home, n., a. & adv. Dwelling house; fixed residence of family or household . . . institution of refuge and rest for destitute or infirm persons . . .

I

When Eleanor and her son Philip moved out they took almost everything with them, leaving Graham only the king-size bed in which his father had died, a black leather sofa suitable for his consulting room (already lined with black leather sofas), his record player and a few odd cups and plastic plates stained with old picnics. This devastation was not, Eleanor asserted, out of revenge. Graham had not been living with them for some weeks, and it was up to her to make a home for the boy, for the children. As the gas cooker was dismantled and borne away in the furniture van, she said, 'After all, he can always buy another one.' Philip found an old dustpan brush and a piece of cardboard and ineffectually swept the gap where the cooker had been.

By mid-morning there was nothing to sit on except the sofa. The moving firm employed nomadic youths, undernourished, asthmatic, wearing great tin medallions. Eleanor remembered moving men like bulls, white-coated, devout with the china, taking a pride in their job. One of the youths sat on the floor and read *Herzog*. Two went out for tea and never came back. Only the foreman, an Italian in wire glasses, worked with conviction. He admired the sofa, and was disappointed to leave it behind.

It became, to Eleanor, a question of keeping the boy's spirits up. For months, ever since she had first seen the new house, her own had been soaring. She had rediscovered energy that she thought had long ago died; at the prospect of living by herself, in her own home, without Graham, without the load of a marriage that had become intolerable, she had felt herself flung helter-skelter, without time to assess or reason, into a life of hope and good sense. She had been unable to sleep at nights, hurrying out of bed to add something more to a list, to write some reminder to herself; or else she had lain on her back, her arms behind her head, smiling at her fantasies and almost unendurably impatient. It seemed at this time incredible to her that she could have endured the last five years of her marriage. She did not even think about it, erasing a quarter of a century of love and passion and habit with plans for curtain rails and bookshelves and where the pictures would hang and what, above all, she would create for her children: after years of anxiety and distress there would once more be a home. She would make it, alone, un-trammelled, a free human being. She imagined that there came a point in one's life where one had to change overnight, be struck by some lightning of truth, or else wither away into some patient, appalling half-death. She believed that she had been struck by this truth; it even electrified her body.

But there was Philip. They sat on the sofa together and she was unable to share all this with him. He was silent, sitting with his elbows on his knees, hair hanging forward, booted feet planted like pedestals. She wanted to explain it all to him, to justify herself, at least to hear him say he was glad they were leaving. She wanted, and intended, to offer him the rest of her life, but the most she could do was forage for a packet of chocolate biscuits in a packing case. He ate two out of politeness. She made a few poor jokes, not worthy of the ebullience she felt. He smiled with his mouth shut, momentarily. At last, before the Italian had finished loading, she suggested that they should go. Philip got up obediently and walked out of the front door of the flat where he had lived for five years, down the stairs, through the main door, down the steps. He opened the door of Eleanor's car, folded himself up and sat waiting.

Eleanor had a curious moment of hesitation about whether or not she should leave her key. Of course she must leave it. She was never coming back. She put it on the bottom of the banisters and slammed the door, going away as easily as though she were going out for a morning's shopping. There was a kind of stab of thought, which had the name and face of Graham. He had left her six weeks ago for some unimaginable life with a twenty-two-year-old person called Nell Partwhistle. Eleanor thought of her as a person because she could not think of her as a girl and did not think of her as a woman; she thought of her as a kind of gap, a nothing. As she started the engine, put the car into gear, released the handbrake, swerved the car out into the road for the last time, she took nothing about Nell Partwhistle seriously, least of all her name. Next week it would be someone else. All that was over and she could put it out of her mind and heart. She remembered Graham saying, 'When we are separated we'll have a huge affair. It's just being married that's so impossible.' Don't remember. Keep going, driving away.

She negotiated the busy main road that led, eventually, out of London.

'I hope I never have to drive down here again,' she said pleasantly.

Philip said nothing.

'It's like the country up there,' she said. 'The blossom's out.'

He muttered something, agreement or comment.

'We must get them to come and do the garden.'

'Yes.'

'I don't know how we've lived so long without a garden.'

He turned his head and looked out of the side window, his sallow face expressionless, the big hands limp on his jeans. He was just fifteen, the youngest. In a minute, he thought, she will offer me sweets and make a home for me; in a minute

9

she will have grown roses round the door and put me in a playpen. He did not have to look at her to know the familiar face glazed with these idiotic dreams, the hair she had not bothered to brush properly this morning, the corduroy sneakers scuffed round the toes, the weight of her grief and optimism. He consciously submitted to her, with loving anger.

'Will they have fixed the cooker?' he asked, with great difficulty.

'No. But I've got an electric kettle.'

'Oh,' he said, admiring her, 'so you bought an electric kettle?'

'Well. I thought it was . . . sensible.'

'Yes. That was very sensible.'

His praise pleased her enormously. She wanted to touch him, stroke his knee or the back of his hairy head, but was afraid of embarrassing him. Although for most of the time she only guessed at his feelings, she had an inordinate respect for them. When he was small she used to lie, out of pride in him, and say that he was the only man she would willingly mend and clean and cook for; the only man whose buttons she would happily sew on. From the look of him, thin and dishevelled, wearing odd socks, and string for a bootlace, this was no longer so. But her respect disabled her from trying to clean him up. Her eldest son Marcus, twenty-five, lived in Paris with a middle-aged theatrical designer called Marcel. She did not think about him very often. The rest of her children were women.

So, out of consideration for Philip's unknown feelings, they drove in silence. She thought about the house they were going to: her house. It was a smaller, older, more elegant version of the one they had lived in for years, when the children were young and she and Graham had made love one night on the dining-room table before, with smooth and smiling efficiency, she had laid it for breakfast. Why, now, remember that? What treacherous lurch of memory brought that up? The death of her sexual life with Graham was a secret disfigurement, a hidden wound that stabbed her without warning in daylight. Don't think about it. It will heal if you don't think about it. There will be others; at least one other. But indulge in that in a minute, when it may become necessary.

'I told you,' she said, 'that Ellis and Gwen are coming round for a drink this evening. To celebrate. And Alex may come.'

'Yes.'

Part of her new life was to include him in her friends, in the numerous friends she would make, giving parties, dinner parties, always answering the telephone ('Not *again*!'), the popular Nell (no, Eleanor) Strathearn, her mantelpiece a continual Christmas. She had no clear idea about how she would set about this transformation, since after a life sentence of marriage she was as isolated, as strange to the world as a released prisoner. She had long ago stopped sharing any kind of life with Graham, except for the occasional dull dinner party when she could be used as a wife. Nevertheless, it was a cheerful fantasy, and driving through dour Kilburn she pulled it up to her chin, nestled inside it, began to smile.

Now she would allow herself to think about him. The well-known story went like this: one day soon her Gaelic knight would telephone, so exquisitely tired and beautiful, urbane and cruel. She would ask him to dinner. The smile spread irresistibly, broadening her chin, filling out the tired hollows.

'The lights were red.' Philip was explaining to her the orchestra of horns coming from immigrants in battered Fords, startled ladies in head-scarves.

'I'm sorry.'

'It would be a fine thing,' he said drily, 'if we never got there.'

Of course, she went on to herself, it could never be a real affair, what with him living in Ireland in all that pomp and ceremony (crumbling eighteenth-century mansion, horses, dogs, hunting would surely be against his principles, some sort of angular, tweeded wife of whom he is still, not knowing me well enough, fond). But he will come to see me when he is in London, and he will find—peace? The prospect of supplying anyone with peace genuinely amused her. The smile became sourer, more intelligent, ran into the contours of her face: I couldn't say that I've ever really specialised in peace.

They were getting nearer. The new key hung, glinting silver, off the bunch of keys swinging from the ignition. They had been together, she and Philip, to buy a dining table, to realise the dinner-party fantasy, and a sofa broad enough and soft enough for making love. He had not, of course, been told the purpose of either.

'Anyway, we'll have a sofa and a table if those hopeless movers never arrive.'

'I'm sure,' he said, with reasonable conviction, 'they will arrive.'

She began looking out at the area in which, probably, she would spend the rest of her life: grimy little shops about to be swallowed by supermarkets; towers of flats, nineteenth-century cottages huddled against their walls; dour pubs, and the blossoming and budding remains of the wood long ago named for St. John. It was ugly, all right. Jessica, visiting it once in her 1928 ball gown and Wellington boots, had commended it for its ugliness. 'It's not pretentious,' she had said, finding a use for her favourite word.

'I wonder when Jessie will . . . come home.'

His grunt, this time, had a downward inflexion. She took it to mean that he doubted whether Jessie, wandering somewhere in the Camargue, would ever come home; or that if she did she would stay; or that if she stayed she would be happy.

'I'm going to buy a piano,' she said, explaining how she would make Jessie happy.

At last, and for the first time, they were there. When she had switched off the engine they sat for a few moments, both looking up at the enigmatic façade of the house, its 'Sold' notice almost obscured by lilac, its uncurtained windows; its air, she invented wildly, of well-mannered repose. Philip glanced at it sourly, with suspicion. For the last four years he had come to think of his school life as the only reality. In December, April and July he came back to an uneasy dream peopled with parents, sisters; occasionally his queer brother Marcus, making no bones about it. Totally isolated, he struggled through it until the time came to wake up, speak, plot, take action. This house might well be a trap. Once inside, the door might slam, imprisoning him for ever.

'Well . . .' she said.

'Well.'

They recognised each other's reluctance. Safe inside the car, they were momentarily conspirators.

'Shall we,' she asked, 'just drive on?'

'Where?'

'I don't know.'

He considered. 'India.'

'Too far.'

They smiled at each other, and Philip concealing his dread, got out of the car and climbed the steps to the front door.

2

It was, on the face of it, a very commonplace story: people meet, love, separate, as often as they are born or die, no one is exempt from some degree of these experiences, however slight. To Graham and Eleanor Strathearn their history had been unique, obsessive, at times sensational. When they met and swiftly married he was an ambitious medical student, she was at art school, waiting for something to happen to her. Graham had been a captain in the R.A.M.C. for a short while, but discovered a shadowy patch on his right lung and sensibly left the Army. Having a head start over most of his contemporaries, the financial assistance of both his mother and mother-in-law, and a natural inclination to live comfortably, he was in partnership in Wimpole Street by the time he was thirty-two. Here he made the most of a couple of inherited actors, and was soon taking swabs from the tender cervixes of minor film stars, pepping up menopausal leading ladies on provincial tours and tranquillising manic-depressive television actors. He was a good, even compassionate, doctor, but as time went on bodies began to bore him and he specialised more and more in drugs to alleviate nervous and emotional disorders. Like so many professional men, his life was split into two unequal parts: authoritative in his consulting room, he could lie on the sofa at home and suck the corner of his handkerchief and refuse to advise his wife or children to take so much as an aspirin. If Eleanor had gone to him as a patient she would have had his infinite concern; since she lived with him as a wife, he depended on her never to let him down, physically or emotionally. It took him a long time to discover that she was as vulnerable as any other woman, and when he did it was a kind of betrayal that he preferred not to recognise. In his professional life nothing, except the mounting disapproval of what he dismissed as antideluvian psychiatrists, stood in his way. He was immensely popular and immensely successful. His patients, nearly all hypochondriacs racked with miseries of heart and mind, carried eighteenth-century snuff-boxes for their innumerable pills and were often, by his apparent devotion to them as much as anything else, comforted.

They had five children, Marcus, Cressida, Daphne, Jessica and, after a long interval and by a joyful mistake, Philip. The relationship between the parents of these growing boys and girls was passionate and intense: that was its weakness. Their marriage was a frail receptacle for all the obsessions and compulsions, the ancient needs and complex demands that go under the name of great love; it had eventually to weaken and break under the strain. For over twenty years, whatever their infidelities, they were consumed by each other. Their life was overloaded with a mutual sexual and emotional need in which affection or respect had very little part. When, after three or four years, Graham started having affairs, cautiously realising his fantasies, they were not wholly consummated until he could present them, sly-eyed and pallid with guilt, to Eleanor. Powerful in her certainty of him, and of herself, she promptly destroyed them, and he was able to feel afraid of her for doing what he had mutely asked her to do. But power can be shaken, and she too became frightened. Very slowly, an imperceptible growth, the fear increased within the love, eating it away. Eleanor's world became terrible with Graham's secrets, Graham's with his deceits. Finally two middle-aged, intelligent, apparently rational human beings became paralysed with terror of each other. The love seemed to have been completely destroyed. They were trying to live in a state in which every shadow threatened, every closed door concealed some unthinkable menace. It was, Eleanor told herself now—hoping to abolish the fear, and the terrible feelings which she could not grapple with—perfectly ridiculous.

That's what her mother would have said; did say. The reason for everything could be found in their mothers. They, not the giggling girls or the occasional inadequate lovers, were the innocent culprits. Mothers, first off the mark at birth, resolutely hanging on for years after the fathers die or disappear, constructing and manipulating, providers of food and love and never enough of either, guilty of appalling excesses and incredible meanness—Mrs. Strathearn in her Kensington apartment with the bridge table laid, and Mrs. Bennet in her country cottage with a consoling view of the churchyard, were the keys to it all. Nobody, least of all Eleanor, a mother herself, realised this. Certainly it never occurred to Mrs. Strathearn with her two no trumps, or to Mrs. Bennet lovingly slashing her roses.

Mrs. Bennet, to begin with, believed in regular meals, regular bowel motions, what she called 'decent' behaviour, gentlemen (public schools, the law, the Church, the medical profession and the Liberal Party), good manners, fair play, John Galsworthy on television and natural compost. She did not believe in sex, machinery, or the independent, unrelated existence of her daughter. While not exactly believing in God—the prospect was a little ridiculous—she was devoted to death, regarding it as the cure for all evils, by which she meant life. However, she remained indomitably alive. Other elderly ladies—at the time of the break-up she was eighty-two—suffered from fluttering hearts, poor eyesight, deafness, arthritis. Mrs. Bennet was healthier than she had been at eighteen, and as much in command of her faculties. She also grew more knowledgeable every year, and was now far better informed about politics, the arts, drug addiction, space travel, sexual permissiveness and other topics of absolutely no use to her than her husband, a gentleman farmer and Justice of the Peace, had ever been.

Eleanor had been brain-washed by this formidably good woman from the moment she had first plucked at her stern nipple and felt, perhaps, her mother's distaste. Although in many ways a rebellious and awkward child—and Mrs. Bennet would be the first to say so—she had grown up with an incurable sense of right and wrong, a passion for order, a rigidity of spirit which made her incapable of appreciating weakness or getting the best out of sin. In her worst nightmares she was desperately trying to clear up a houseful of muddle and dirt, ineffectually trying to organise chaos. The idea that life could be enjoyable had seemed, for many years, a kind of blasphemy. Life was like a room in which one hardly dared move for fear of tripping over rules, blundering into shibboleths, breaking some valuable regulation. Every movement she made seemed to produce disorder, and her mother's melancholy, uncomplaining disapproval. 'What are we going to do about Nelly?' Mrs. Bennet would sigh, whenever the child shouted or wept or kicked against what Mrs. Bennet called the pricks. Around the age of twelve Eleanor took to cleaning her bedroom in the middle of the night, sweeping and polishing as though exorcising some devil. This was the only one of her eccentricities that Mrs. Bennet could understand.

It did not occur to Eleanor for many years that she might not love her mother. Owing to Mrs. Bennet's unstinting efforts, the two women were so similar on the surface that Eleanor did not really think of herself as having a separate identity. The question of loving or not loving did not therefore arise. For most of Eleanor's adult life, though living apart from each other, they had cooked the same wholesome food, eaten at four regular intervals throughout the day; they had furnished their houses with the same unpretentious good taste and complete disregard for their husbands; they had been reliable, competent and energetic. The secrets that Eleanor had been forced to keep from her mother—aberrations of heart and soul, like fear, love, passion, the onset of intelligence—had, not finding an outlet, congealed and set in inextricable confusion. This was where her nightmares came from, the acres of cobwebs, the rotting floors, the impossibility of matching up roomfuls of odd socks and broken china. In these nightmares Mrs. Bennet appeared hostile, cruel and—worst of all—downright ineffectual. The mother who could manage everything, support everyone, make order out of the worst chaos, became, in her dreams, useless.

In marrying Mrs. Bennet by way of her daughter, Graham seemed to have found the perfect doctor's wife. He did not at first realise the discrepancy between Eleanor and her mother. He thought that he was going to be looked after, like the children, for the rest of his life. Even at the height of his uxoriousness, when Eleanor entirely possessed him, he dreamed of asking her permission to go to bed with someone else, of bringing his mistresses home to nursery tea in full assurance of her blessing. She let him down by being jealous, vain and unreasonable. Her secret self, of whom he became so afraid, was capable of the most appalling atrocities, such as not giving her permission for him to go to bed with anyone else, and actively withholding her blessing. The more her inconsistency baffled him, the more oppressed he became by the competence and discipline on which he had once relied; the more successful he became, the more confidence he felt in rebelling against Mrs. Bennet. The mere prospect of roast beef and Yorkshire pudding sent him rushing out in his Porsche to some non-existent patient. The idea of sitting at home in the evening, the threat of Eleanor's confusion breaking through Mrs. Bennet's favourite television programme, created a plethora of conferences which he absolutely had to attend, a score of would-be suicides who needed him desperately until four in the morning, or occasionally all night. Secretly, with a good deal of planning and expenditure, he built up a small private army to defend himself against the dangers of home : actresses, models, car salesmen, restaurateurs, anyone of whom the Bennets (they were also snobs) would disapprove. At the same time he became incapable of so much as touching his wife, remembering his passion for her with guilty distaste, as though he had been guilty of incest. They slept apart, and until Nell Partwhistle turned up to make him feel permissibly incestuous his life was, as he oftened complained, intolerably difficult.

For much of this Mrs. Strathearn, whose name Eleanor had taken, was equally responsible. A small, wispy, attractive woman, she had been vaguely intellectual in her youth and married a schoolmaster. He, inheriting a moderate income, had started a preparatory school of his own on the South Coast and died at the age of fifty-five, leaving Mrs. Strathearn with enough to live on and to finish the education of their only son. Mrs. Strathearn did not like children. In fact, her sparse flesh crept when she was in contact with them. Apart from her considerable devotion to her husband, the years at the preparatory school had been hell. Graham was looked after by a succession of nursemaids and was left behind in the holidays, during which his parents made trips to Italy, Greece, the Black Forest and the Dordogne. This placid antipathy continued until the schoolmaster died and Mrs. Strathearn became aware that Graham was fifteen. She then made overtures to him—hand-made ties, trips to the theatre and opera, holidays abroad—but it was too late. Something might have been salvaged between them if he had become—or, more accurately, remained—a homosexual. She would have liked that. But the Army corrupted him and he began his lifelong search for a mother/sister, tearing through A.T.S. in Sam Browne belts and red lipsticks at the rate of one a week. When he married Eleanor—then arrogant and hesitant, tough and yielding, perpetually surprising him by the fact that she was all he had ever wanted—Mrs. Strathearn revived her bridge,

19

bought a Siamese cat and settled into an elegant, totally self-obsessed old age.

She had given him nothing, apart from paying for his education. He was the complete opposite of Eleanor—a self-made man with no criteria, no points of reference, no judgement to go by except that sketched on his outer skin at school. He was free of any sense of obligation or loyalty, innocently selfish, naively indulgent. Even his cruelty was inadvertent. His mind was excellent, but he could very seldom make it up since he was incapable of assessing the consequences. He learned to disguise this disadvantage by calling his mind 'open'. His tastes, uncertain as they were, were known as 'catholic'. Apart from his relationship with Eleanor, he could be content with life; apart from Eleanor, it could be very easy. Eleanor thought that she was the only person in the world who believed him to be capable of suffering; in Mrs. Bennet's book this was a virtue. He saw no virtue in it; directly Eleanor had convinced him that it might be true he took the second decision of his life and moved out. He did not actually say that he was moving out, and took nothing with him. He just didn't come back. Eleanor packed his clothes and sent them, for lack of anywhere else, to Wimpole Street. She then telephoned him and informed him that he had left home. He accepted her analysis of the situation and agreed, realising that he ought to feel guilty, to buy her a house. Both Mrs. Strathearn and Mrs. Bennet were, in their different ways, gratified. Although the marriage had lasted for twenty-six years, they told themselves and their dearest friends that they had always known it would never work out.

As for the children, the first three, born and growing while Graham was getting established, were Bennets. This was during Eleanor's sovereignty, while her chief counsellor was still her mother. Like herself, they were imbued with conscience and liberally supplied with guilt. Graham, though an affectionate man, found them almost unrecognisable as they grew older. Inconsistently—for he found nothing wrong

20

in it—he blamed Eleanor for the fact that Marcus had turned out to be a homosexual, though at the same time he was thankful. Marcus was extremely good-looking, and the competition would have been embarrassing. As it was, with Marcus happily living abroad, he seldom found it necessary to admit to anyone that he had a twenty-five-year-old son. Marcus hated his father with Bennet-like vigour, but, of the two grandmothers, greatly preferred Mrs. Strathearn. Eleanor moved him so unbearably that his only salvation was to keep away. When he was with her he sometimes thought that his inability to protect her would drive him mad.

Marcus, with Mrs. Bennet's financial assistance, had been to Eton and Cambridge; from the age of thirteen, therefore, she had left him alone, trusting that he would learn good manners and a sense of decency elsewhere. Cressida and Daphne, being women, were fair game. Grudgingly admitting that they were technically Graham's daughters as well as Eleanor's, and that he (of course) loved them, she assaulted them with ponies, and tweed coats with velvet collars, and puddings and syrup of figs and hymns (religion was good for children) and brisk walks whatever the weather; she knitted stout socks for them, taught them to sew square beads round the edges of cork mats and to say thank you and to ask before they got down from table. When they came home from staying with Mrs. Bennet and Graham said 'fuck' or 'bloody' in front of them they blushed delicately and tittered with lowered heads. They lived, as Eleanor had done, secretly, storing up unhappiness until they were old enough to feel it.

They were pretty and feminine and amusing: Graham adored them both until, within two years of each other, they became sixteen, then seventeen, then old, then older than many of the girls with whom he spent his difficult evenings. There were rows, scenes, shocking eruptions of jealousy and resentment and sexual anger. Both girls left home, Cressida with an actor to a room in Golders Green, Daphne to a provincial university. They never went back. Eleanor saw them frequently, and they took their lovers down to Buckingham-shire for Mrs. Bennet's approval, which was never whole-hearted. But the break-up of the home had begun.

Perhaps Mrs. Bennet was satiated with Cressida and Daphne. Even she was growing older, though not at the same rate as the rest of them. Perhaps Graham was more dismayed by his apparent failure with his elder children than he would admit. Certainly Eleanor was slipping, losing faith. In any case, Jessica, three years younger than Daphne, was a changeling in the Bennet world. She clung to her father and resisted every attempt to bring her up well, or indeed bring her up at all. Daunted as a child by her sisters' good marks, glossy plaits and easy chatter, she became very quiet and vague, never quite sure if it was night or morning, easily frightened, mothering a vast family of dolls and mops and stones. As time went on, Eleanor began to think that Jessica was probably a genius. Graham, doting and negligent, said of course. More frequently she was desolated by the girl's lack of order, as though Jessica had been born to realise her worst nightmares. The idea of creating a home for Jessica was secretly rather alarming. She was not at all sure that Jessica —who slept on the floor, fenced in by a great brass bedstead —really wanted a home, or if she did whether it necessarily included Eleanor. No one had suggested that the girl should stay with Graham. It was assumed that Graham could not manage her, what with Nell Partwhistle and his new distaste for family life. Jessica was in fact delighted by the separa-tion, which she thought long overdue; for the rest, she kept her thoughts to herself, obediently threw eighteen years' ac-cumulation of possessions into trunks, suitcases, baskets, cardboard boxes and carriers and went off to the Camargue with a toothbrush in the back pocket of her jeans, a guitar, and two cartons of yoghurt in a paper bag.

All these people—even Mrs. Strathearn, in her way—loved Philip. It was a responsibility he could hardly bear. He had been the ostensible reason for holding them all more or less together for so long. He was now the reason (even Eleanor couldn't think of another) for making a new home, though it might, to some, have seemed rather late in the day. He was heartily sick of being the reason for everything, but he had great compassion for the lot of them and wanted to do his best. He was the one child whom Graham had grown old enough to love as a father, with a small sense of responsibility and without reservation. Philip's love for Graham was also fatherly, a protective, indulgent affection for a man who was not quite his equal. His feelings for Eleanor were even stronger and more complex than those of his elder brother. Sometimes he hated her, and this was even harder to bear than the love. He had learned to live very much alone, preserving himself so that when he went back to school there would be something left. As in a family tree, he was not the final, triumphal flower at the top, but the small root at the bottom, supporting the whole cumbersome growth from underground.

When Eleanor and Philip opened the front door and stepped into the empty hall they were not alone. The house was already inhabited.

3

By early evening the Italian, having acquired more help from somewhere, had dumped all the furniture in the wrong places and gone home. Philip had briefly gone to look at his room, been disheartened and come away. Surrounded by tottering piles of books, crates of china, tables and chairs standing awkwardly about like guests in a strange house, there suddenly seemed nothing to do. Mrs. Bennet's spirit had temporarily deserted them. They sat exhausted, inert, guiltily aware of failing each other, waiting for the celebratory guests to arrive.

Cressida, staying in Virginia with her elderly American lover, had sent a cable saying firmly: 'Happy House'. Daphne had taken someone down to the country for Mrs. Bennet's approval, but sent flowers. Mrs. Bennet herself provided a card on which 'Bless This House' was inscribed in Gothic lettering. None of them were there to help. The telephone squatted on the floor like a yellow frog. Above all else, Eleanor longed to telephone Graham and say help me. Above all else, Philip longed to say to her I will help you, but didn't know how.

Alex arrived half an hour early, clattering through the front door like a galvanised windmill, giving her a great kiss on the mouth and shaking Philip's limp hand as though hoping to wring something from him. 'Well!' he said. 'Well! Isn't this splendid?' He whirled about, looking for something splendid, found the champagne and opened it manfully with a bang and a spurt and a decisive rush towards the grouped glasses. Both Eleanor's personal friends were her ex-lovers. She had been away for occasional weekends with Alex while Graham was abroad, and had filled in many solitary evenings with him when Graham was somewhere in London. For a short while, at the beginning of the affair, she had felt herself to be in love with him; when she got to know him better she began to love him a little for his good intentions, and because he loved her with as much passion and tenderness as he could. When they both realised that through some incurable perversity she would rather wait through the night for Graham than sleep soundly in Alex's bed, they gave up love altogether and resorted to what Eleanor imagined must be friendship. In her plans, or fantasies, for her new life, she relied on him heavily. He was what Mrs. Bennet called, with suspicion, a confirmed bachelor ('He's not at all ... *odd*, dear, is he?'), a successful business man, a theatre-goer and music-lover and *Times* leader reader, a happy, generous, often ebullient, fellow, who was still at this time terrified of the idea of being possessed. Eleanor had never tried to possess him, because she didn't want to. She did not realise his misgivings over the fact that she was at last alone and, presumably, available.

'It's smashing, darling,' he said. 'Great. Here's to you.'

She turned in a sudden unexpected cavern of loneliness and uncertainty and smiled in his direction, raising her glass. 'Thank you.'

He leaned over and grasped her grubby knee. 'You've done it,' he said earnestly. 'Good girl, good girl.'

Philip stirred his champagne with his finger, watching the bubbles. Done what? His thumb hovered towards his mouth; instead, he took a gulp of the awful drink and looked round the room with what he hoped was bright attention. He didn't want to let her down, but he longed, suddenly, to telephone his father. Sooner or later they would expect him to say something. He was in agony. He thought of himself saying ' 'Allo, 'allo, 'allo' in a Cockney accent on the telephone, pretending that nothing was wrong.

'Well, what d'you think of your new home, Philip?' Alex asked him heartily. He sounded as though he were cuffing the boy over the head, which on many occasions he would like to do.

'Lovely,' Philip muttered.

'Better than that gloomy flat, eh?'

Philip made a desperate sound, which might have meant anything. Eleanor thought she knew what it meant and came rushing to the rescue, pulling herself together as she rushed.

'Ellis and Gwen are coming. I thought we might all go out to dinner, there's nothing to eat here, we're both starving . . .'

'Can't.' Alex had once been in analysis and had learned from his analyst to deal with all improper demands in a clear and unambivalent manner. When he realised that Eleanor, who momentarily couldn't speak, was not going to ask him why, or where he was going, or with whom, he offered, 'I promised to take some people to the theatre. Sorry.'

'Oh well . . .' Devastated by his treachery, she sounded thoroughly light-hearted. 'Another time.'

.   .   .   .   .

Graham called in at the flat at about six o'clock, having cancelled his last three appointments: to one, he told his secretary to say that he had suddenly been called abroad; to another, that he had an urgent consultation with his dentist; to the third, an unimportant poet with delirium tremens, he gave no excuse at all. His terror of Eleanor had congealed, today, into an ominous anger. He took three tranquillisers before he left Wimpole Street, and drove with extreme care.

He had not, of course, expected Eleanor and Philip to be there. He knew that they had moved, and had once or twice imagined them putting suitcases into the boot of her car, and felt relieved that he hadn't been there to carry them. He took the letters that had come by the second post out of the box, glanced at them, noted that they were uninteresting and put them back in the box. Then he jogged briskly up the stairs, jangling his keys. He intended to move back here now they had gone, out of his furnished flat which was cramped and expensive.

The impact was not immediate. At first he merely noted that something was wrong, drifts of shavings and old newspapers on the floor, a curious degree of light. It was the presence of the sofa, long and narrow and hard and black, that made him realise there was no other furniture in the room. His tranquillity deserted him. 'Bitch!' he said aloud. 'Bitch!' He pounded upstairs. His bed, without sheets or blankets, stood alone, pale patches on the walls where chest of drawers, tables, pictures had been. He stared about him like a man whose city has been ruined overnight. He ran downstairs. At the sight of the gap where the gas cooker had been—the old dustpan brush and piece of cardboard nearby—he shouted 'Christ!' and lunged for the telephone. Then he realised that he did not know his wife's telephone number. He rang his solicitor, Humphrey Push, who was working late.

'The bitch has taken everything, every damn thing!'

'Well . . . didn't you discuss it?'

'Discuss it?'

'Come to an arrangement,' Push said, sounding like Mrs. Bennet.

'You don't have a discussion,' Graham said, 'with a bloody burglar. There's not a chair. Not even a piece of soap. She's taken the gas cooker.'

'I suppose she had to furnish the house,' Push said feebly. 'Did you make any provision . . . give her any money . . . to furnish the house?'

'My God, I bought the bloody place, didn't I?'

'True . . .'

'Well, what can I do? Can I get it back?'

There was a momentary pause, a tiny click, an exhaling of smoke.

'I think you've got to face it, old chap. It's a sizable house, and she's got the children.'

'Children!' Graham wheeled round on his heel, imploring the devastated room, abandoned at last by the Bennets. 'There aren't any children! They're all antique, out on their own! The boy's away at school . . .'

'Nevertheless,' Push said, smoothly puffing, 'your wife's house is what you might call . . . the home.'

'And what about me?' Graham yelled over forty-five years. 'I've got nothing! I'm left with nothing!'

'If I were you,' Push said, 'I would go back to that nice little girl and get her to pour you a stiff drink, and call me in the morning.'

'She's such a bitch,' Graham said.

'Who?'

'Nelly. Eleanor. My fucking wife.'

'They always are,' Push said.

When he put the receiver down it was getting dark. The empty flat was very unpleasant. A small part of him wanted to huddle down on the floor and go to sleep, perhaps in the night he would be covered with leaves and found years later, emaciated. He pulled himself together and left it, forgetting to take the letters out of the box.

In his furnished flat, full of tallboys and Burmese trays and renovated oil lamps, Nell Partwhistle was waiting by the gas fire like a kitten. Like a kitten, she stood up, arched herself for his perfunctory kiss, and walked delicately away to her bowl of onion-flavoured crisps. He flung everything down everywhere, coat, attaché-case, brief-case. He asked if anyone had telephoned. She shook her head.

'She's taken everything, the bitch,' he said, pouring himself a drink.

Nell looked at him wonderingly.

He telephoned his Answering Service and listened, impassive, to three urgent messages. I can't cope, he said to himself, and picked up two handfuls of Nell's limp hair. She looked at him and smiled. He squeezed the hair in his fists and, because it had no nerves, tugged it a little. She continued to smile.

'What's for supper?' he asked.

She shrugged, smiling, rearranging her hair like a drape in a shop window.

He went to the kitchen and made himself a Welsh rarebit, Philip's favourite. While it was still under the grill, browning nicely, the telephone rang. Nell sat plaiting the ends of her hair, gazing dreamily into the gas fire. He answered it abruptly, caring deeply for the burning cheese.

'Hallo?'

' 'Allo, 'allo, 'allo . . .' The voice broke high on the last syllable.

'Philip.' Joy came over him. 'Where are you?'

'I'm at . . . the new house. I thought I'd phone you. Just to see how you're getting on.'

'I'm getting on fine. How are you?' He mimed urgently that Nell should go and look at the Welsh rarebit. She smiled, turning towards the fire, and slowly, strand by strand, piling her hair on top of her head.

'I'm fine.'

'How's the house?'

'It's lovely.'

'Well . . . how are you, then? When am I going to see you?'

'I don't know.'

'Why not come to supper tomorrow?' He wondered quickly whether he could be back in time to cook supper, and put it out of his mind. The cheese was burning. He silently implored Nell Partwhistle's back.

'Well . . . I don't know. I don't know what Mother's doing.'

'Will you ring me, then?'

'Where?'

'Wimpole. In the morning.'

'All right. I've got a phone in my bedroom, actually.'

'That's good. Ring me in the morning then.'

'All right.'

'Good night, Phil. Lots of love.'

'Good night.'

A kind of remote sadness, like an echo or an omen, came over Graham as he put the receiver down. He sighed, and went to rescue the cheese. As he was tipping it on to a plate, he realised that he still didn't know their telephone number, and that he could have talked to Eleanor about the furniture. Tomorrow would do.

'I have to go out,' he said, as he stretched in the brocaded armchair, the Welsh rarebit balanced on his stomach.

Nell Partwhistle smiled as she yawned, letting her hair fall over his knee in matted knots.

.   .   .   .   .

Philip had gone upstairs to telephone his father after Ellis and Gwen arrived and there was nowhere to sit and he could safely leave his champagne without Alex making some shameful comment. He quite liked these friends of his mother's, but they were old and boisterous, he preferred young, quiet people. The telephone conversation had not been satisfactory and he felt cut off from the world through some inadequacy of his own. He set up his record player on a packing case and sat on the floor listening to Simon and Garfunkel, chewing the end of his hair and missing something that had not yet happened.

Ellis was a great mass of a man who wore a thin man's face, deeply grooved and deprived. He was a talented painter in the Francis Bacon style, great howls out of darkness, but for himself preferred his neat, unkindly little cartoons, seventeenth-century chamber music and orderly people, particularly the rich. He had been born forty-six years ago in Middlesbrough, the son of a railway clerk and an art teacher, and over the years had come to think of himself as working class. In fact his working-class origins were as vague as many people's pretensions to belong, way back and infinitely indirectly, to the Churchills or Wellingtons or tenth cousins of the Royal Family. As they might display some plastic coat of arms, or cherish a chipped snuff-box with indecipherable initials, so Ellis wore peasant clothes—they happened to be French peasant clothes, outrageous to Middlesbrough—and spoke with an indeterminate Northern accent. He would sometimes admit to having done rather well at his local grammar school, where he had recently presented the prizes—the first time he had been further north than Highgate in twenty-seven years. Until he was forty he was constantly getting married; now he lived with quiet, intelligent girls whom he brought up and educated and who inevitably deserted him. When sober, he was terrifyingly polite, behaving with the strained diffidence of a small boy at a tea party who fears a thrashing if he drops the scones. When drunk, he hit everything in sight, including people; he loved and wept and shouted and blundered about like an uncontrolled robot. Eleanor preferred him drunk, in spite of the damage. When he was drunk she could put her arms round him and he would lie inert, washed up on the beach of her shoulder.

They had met at a private showing of one of his exhibitions, during his final marriage. He was the first person she had known who went straight through the Bennet façade—knocking it about fairly carelessly on the way—and settled down in her confusion as though perfectly at home there. At first it was an enormous relief. They made little effort to hide the affair from Graham, and none whatever to hide it from the anonymous and rapidly vanishing wife. Graham, who felt perfectly secure with Eleanor, appeared to find it amusing; the wife, on her way out, threatened both suicide and murder. One evening Ellis lumbered into the house and asked Graham for Eleanor's hand in marriage. Graham gave him many drinks and patted him on the back and before long Graham and Eleanor went to bed, and made love, leaving the huge man propped up on the sofa like a giant glassy-eyed doll. They were both very fond of him, and in the morning Graham's first thought was to take him Alka-Seltzer.

They went on seeing each other for a while, but Eleanor's hopeless longing for order crept irresistibly back and she began to want to tidy Ellis away. His demands were too great; he was too big, too inert, too unmanageable, she was full up already with Graham and the children and her private chaos, she had no room for him. They began to quarrel, he called her a bourgeois bitch, she, not meaning it, called him a phoney layabout. One day, outside a pub where they had met for a recriminatory beer, she got into her car and slammed the door and left him, she thought, for ever.

It was her affection for him, serenely untroubled by all these amateur dramatics, that kept the relationship half alive over the next ten years, and transformed it, in the end, into a kind of friendship. Because of this persistence and what might have seemed loyalty, Ellis felt for her a kind of wary awe, almost a reverence, which she found unwelcome. She would rather, now, be hugged and buffeted, as in the old days. It had occurred to her that some of the liveliness might revive between them now that she was alone.

Gwen had started living with him while she was still at school, and was now, from the look of her tense, ageless face, the plaiting of bony fingers in her lap, the sense she gave of being about to spring away, ready for graduation. Eleanor felt a particular affection for her because, being so vulnerable, she was so contained; being so continually hurt, she was so unscathed. She was a mysterious girl with the appearance of a young Virginia Woolf, equine, nervous, draped in a rather gloomy dress.

Ellis was sober this evening, which was a pity. He had packed himself neatly into a small chair and covered himself with a kind of dogged melancholy. He knew that this was supposed to be the occasion of Eleanor's emancipation, but found it all pretty meaningless. Gwen had a doleful eye on him as he accepted a third glass of champagne; she was terrified of his drinking and was already gathering herself to run away. Alex chattered easily, but kept looking at his watch. Eleanor forced herself to drink, in the ludicrous hope that it might make her feel better.

'Shall you mind living here alone?' Ellis asked cautiously.

'I don't think so.' She sounded as though she had considered the problem and come to a conclusion. 'I've never lived alone in my life,' she said, making a faint effort to be more truthful. 'I suppose it's about time. . . .'

'It's the only way,' Alex said briskly, dreading any possible demand for sympathy or support. 'Come home in the evening, shut the door, turn on some music, flop down on the sofa. Ah, it's bliss.'

They all three looked at him with startled disbelief.

'Don't answer the telephone,' he went on, rather wildly. 'Get into your pyjamas. The hell with everyone.' He looked at his watch.

'No . . .' Ellis considered, 'that's not for me. I need someone. It doesn't much matter who it is. But I do need someone.'

'So do I,' Gwen said quietly, adding the final touch to the conversation. They put it aside and started another one, about the production of some play that only Alex had seen. Muttering something about tidying herself up, Eleanor left them.

The house seemed large because it was on four floors; most of the space was taken up with stairs, landings, a hallway that the estate agents had called gracious; there were comparatively few rooms. Most of the lights had no bulbs—anyway, she didn't yet know where the switches were—and she groped her way down to Philip's basement, tracking her hand along the cold, unfamiliar wall, stumbling and almost falling on the curve of the stairs. He had by now fixed up a couple of lamps and hung his curtains. He looked almost cosy. She had been prepared to try to comfort him, if necessary. She now realised that of the two of them he, at the moment, was more of a Bennet.

'Well,' she asked. 'How are you?'

'All right. How are you?'

She allowed herself a rare moment of honesty. 'I feel . . . strange.'

'Yes,' he said. 'Is there any loo paper?'

'Somewhere. I'll find you some.'

'It's all right,' he said. 'I'll look for it.'

She was sitting on his school trunk. He would go back in a week's time. She couldn't mention it or think about it, the parting seemed devastating. Was this any way to set up home, with this sudden anguish and lassitude? What had happened, in the course of the day, to the fantasies that had enlivened her over the past two months, the plans, the lists, the organisation, the flying hither and thither with bits of twig and mud and rubbish? She was behaving like a child who, exhausted with the prospect of Christmas, sits howling among his new toys in a desolation of grief. Such a child would be given a stern talking-to by Mrs. Bennet, then comforted, given cocoa and put early to bed. With a deep sense of relief, she reached for Philip's telephone.

'Mother?'

'Is that you, Nelly? Daphne's just left. I thought the young man very odd. How did the move go?'

'Will you come and stay?'

'Come and stay?' Was there actually a hesitation, the slightest reluctance? 'Well, darling, if you think I can be of any use . . . I'm rather feeble, you know . . .' (Liar.) 'I don't know that I should be able to do much to help . . . Still, of course, if you need me . .'

'Can you come tomorrow?'

'Tomorrow? Well, I was going to plant out the dahlias, but I suppose Franco can do that. Yes,' nobly. 'Yes, of course I'll come tomorrow.'

'I'll meet you. Can you catch the eleven-fifteen?'

'Very well, dear.'

The moment she put the receiver down, the telephone rang again, surprising them both. They both knew it must be Graham and watched it, Philip with longing, Eleanor with dread, as it rang.

'You answer it,' Eleanor said.

He growled 'Hullo', waited, then passed the receiver over to her.

'It's for you.'

'Who is it?'

'I don't know.'

'Eleanor? Patrick.'

'Patrick . . . ?'

'Kilcannon. Remember me?'

'Of course . . .' To Philip's amazement she lit up, all the dark and shadow shone with immediate light, she was refulgent like a tall building; she glittered. 'How are you?'

'Oh . . . not well. Anyway, I don't want to bother you with that. How are you placed on the evening of the ninth? I thought I might come and take a drink off you.'

'The ninth? When is the ninth?' She sounded like someone merrily looking for a pin in an untidy work-basket. 'Anyway, it doesn't matter. I shall be placed'—she was daring to mock him a little—'exactly here.'

'I'm sorry to make plans so far in advance. But I shall be coming over that day . . .'

'Coming over?'

'From Ireland.'

'Oh, yes . . . of course. Come about seven. I'll give you a steak.' She knew, as she said it, that it was the most obscene way of telling him that she would give him herself.

'Well, I may not be there until eight. Will that do?'

'That,' she said, 'will do wonderfully.'

'Goodbye, then. See you on the ninth.'

'Yes. Goodbye.'

She could not help whirling on Philip and, much to his pleased astonishment, hugging him as though she had just met him again after a long absence.

'Who was that?' he asked.

She regained her balance, her dreadful sense of suitability. Instead of saying simply 'Patrick Kilcannon' or, absurdly, 'My Gaelic knight', she spoke to him as though he were a child.

'The nicest man I know,' she said.

She didn't wait to savour the bad taste of this remark. Alex was calling from upstairs, 'Are you there? I'm off!'

She shouted carelessly, 'I'm on the phone! Thank you for coming! See you soon!' The front door slammed as she dialled Mrs. Bennet's number.

'Mother? Look, I'm sorry. I was in a panic. It's all right, you needn't come tomorrow. Come later, when it's more comfortable.'

'Well, darling . . . are you sure? I would like to get the dahlias in . . .'

'Absolutely sure.'

'You can manage all right?'

'I can manage perfectly.'

Gorgeously clothed in fantasy, serene and animated and resolute, she took Philip's arm and led him upstairs to rescue Ellis and Gwen from their motiveless celebration.

4

She had met Patrick Kilcannon once, three months ago, and
had never seen him since. It had been at a party given by one
of Graham's most distinguished patients, an elderly and
beautiful actress who assumed that everyone was married in
some shape or form, so included wives in all invitations, even
those to her most intimate homosexual friends. Eleanor had
opened theirs—to Dr. and Mrs. Graham Strathearn—before
Graham could hide or destroy it. Although she knew at the
time about Nell Partwhistle, she did not know that in another
few days Graham would be leaving. He was being exceptionally affectionate just then, even to the point of carelessly asking her to spend the night with him—'You can come and
sleep with me if you like.' She had not accepted the offer,
being too proud, or hurt, or stupid, or sceptical of free gifts.
But in a moment of optimism she decided to go to the party
with him, and since her decision had some of the old Bennet
vigour he had nervously agreed.

It was a dull affair in a splendid suite of rooms, the bright
chandeliers hot on the bald pates of theatrical dignitaries, the
champagne warm, the food indifferent. Graham, whose
knowledge of many of the guests was extremely intimate,
moved from group to group as though doing the round of a

very exclusive hospital ward. The actress, bearing Patrick Kilcannon on her arm, suddenly decided to drop him off on Eleanor.

'Sir Patrick Kilcannon,' the actress murmured. 'Of course you know . . .' She flew off in a whirl of chiffon, her elbows pressed to her sides to facilitate speed.

'I'm sorry . . . ?' he asked.

'Strathearn. Eleanor Strathearn.'

He was short—later, in her fantasies, he became at least a foot taller—and dapper in a rather old-fashioned way, his clothes had been made to last, and were well cared for. He was rather too handsome, almost a stereotype, with the regular, aquiline features that smoulder in the illustrations to women's magazine stories. He had greying hair and a deeply attentive manner. Eleanor fell in love.

Unlike Graham she was not prone to falling in love. Her affairs with Alex and Ellis, although unusually interesting at times, had been in a sense obligatory, domestic, and lacking in ecstasy. This was largely because she had been in love with Graham, and had little energy to spare. Now, unexpectedly, tumultuously, as easily as stepping off a church steeple, she lost her reason. He took her hand to lead her to the supper table. She followed him like a dazed child, walking carefully. They stood, hand in hand, looking at appalling hams and turkeys dressed up like birthday cake. Since he was making her laugh, he was no doubt witty. He provided her with food, and unhesitatingly led her to a smaller room, where they sat on two small gilt chairs with their knees touching and talked, she thought, about pollution and co-education and the situation in Belfast. Other people joined them for a few moments; like royalty, they sat on their gold chairs, and politely listened, and turned to each other again with relief and renewed pleasure. After a while he noticed an empty sofa, which they occupied. His arm fell loosely and naturally across her shoulders. He was not, he said, a happy man. He had grave responsibilities, difficulties, complications in his life, but he wouldn't bore her with them now. She sat within his arm, doting on him but talking a great deal, as though he had oiled the whole mechanism of speech and thought and feeling. His wife, he said, seldom came over to England, he had one daughter, who was doing voluntary work in West Africa. The more he revealed a noble melancholy, the more enchanted she became. She wanted to go upstairs with him immediately and find a bed and take him into the protective custody of her body.

When he said my God, it was late, he must go, she looked round for Graham, but he had disappeared. She asked Kilcannon to drive her home. He said he didn't have a car, but they would share a taxi. Then he asked her the first and only question about herself: was she alone? She laughed and said she appeared to be.

In the taxi, awkward though it was, they kissed, hugged, stroked, caressed in a passion of impatience. After a while he began to apologise, saying that he had a service flat, but he was very well known there. . . . Yes, she said, she understood. It was impossible for him to come up to Graham's flat. She thought of suggesting that they went to an hotel, but guessed, rightly, that there was a limit to his impulsiveness. They sat a little apart, he straightened his tie and palmed his hair down.

'Can I see you again?'

She laughed at the ridiculous question. 'Yes.'

'When?'

'Any time. Any time.'

The taxi stopped. He had an afterthought. If she wanted to contact him, he said, she should write to his club. 'I have to go back tomorrow, but I'll be over again in three weeks. I'll ring you.' They kissed again, and she got out of the taxi and ran up the front steps without looking back. Graham was still out. She beamed at herself in the mirror, telling herself: I have a lover.

The next day she realised that she had not given him her telephone number, nor, Mrs. Bennet's voice reminded her

39

tartly, had he asked for it. She wrote a short note to his club, and ten days later received a reply from Galway: 'Thank you for the number. It turned out to be one of those remarkable evenings, much to my enchanted surprise. Although I don't think I care terribly much for those theatrical soirées. I am in for a fairly bloody time in the next couple of weeks —estate troubles and so on, which I won't bore you with, and a series of engagements of quite stunning tedium. But I would like to descend on you for a drink one evening on my next trip to London. May I telephone? Love, Patrick.'

In the meanwhile Graham had left, the reality of her pain, loneliness and humiliation had become inescapable. She drove herself into finding the house, bullied herself into believing in it. Kilcannon did not write or telephone; in a way she was relieved, because during this time she felt old and ugly, almost deformed with unhappiness, incapable either of loving or being loved. She thought of him frequently, as though he were some sort of reward reserved for the future, when she would be miraculously autonomous, free and revived. She had told Cressida and Daphne most of the story of their meeting, and it was the young women, huddled delightedly over their instant coffee, longing to feel that she was being taken care of and sexually occupied, who christened him the Gaelic knight, equipping him with white charger, armour, visor and a monumental spear. Eleanor giggled with them, with a hollow heart. When Philip came home for the Easter holidays they bought the sofa as a secret gift.

Two days before they moved, and three months after they had met, he wrote again, this time from his club: 'My dear Eleanor . . . I have telephoned you a couple of times, but the calls have proved abortive. I am writing to see if we can bridge the gulf that seems to have opened. I shall be in London for about ten days now and I would love to have a drink and a cosy little chat about the Irish question or something. The most likely time for me looks like Wednesday evening. If this would appeal to you I suggest you telephone me at the club and we can talk. For the rest my programme in London looks more than usually depressing. Love, Patrick.'

It was too soon. She did not telephone, but wrote that she was moving house on Thursday, so that on Wednesday there would be nowhere to sit and probably nothing to drink. Also, she said, Philip would be home, although he had no idea who Philip was. She said there was no gulf, but not how much she wanted to see him and be comforted and brought back from the dead. She asked him to telephone her at the new house, where, she said, she would be alone. She gave him no help in trying to understand her situation, because it seemed to her that her situation was nothing to do with him. In her new life—which she thought of as ready-made, overlooking the necessity for rebirth and long, arduous development—he would have an inordinate importance. She was content to wait.

.　　.　　.　　.　　.

She kept a child's blackboard in the kitchen on which she chalked reminders and messages to herself. That night, before she went to bed in the strange bedroom, after Ellis and Gwen had gone and Philip was asleep, she wrote 'Patrick 9th' at the top of the board, underlined it and propped it against the wall. It was her first energetic act since they had arrived, and a challenge to all the sorrow she had left behind. For the first time in months she did not mourn for Graham before she slept. There were only three and a half weeks before the ninth and there was a lot to do. Even the thought of Philip going away did not deject her. On the magical, inevitable ninth she would share a bed again, revive her skill, remember the keen delights of generosity, she would be loved. She held her pillow like a doll, and went to sleep smiling.

5

Daphne came round the following evening on her way home from work. She was a big, melancholy, remarkably beautiful girl, a true Bennet and a martyr to her own efficiency. Six months ago she had answered an advertisement in the Women's Appointments of *The Times*: 'Well-known Writer requires good-humoured, reliable P.A./Secretary. Varied and demanding work involving occasional periods abroad. Driving licence. Theatre or film-world experience an asset. £25 p.w.' She had got the job because the writer's wife had summed her up as being sexually reliable, in spite of her looks. Shortly afterwards, the writer's wife had left him for their local builder, who was young and energetic and could put up shelves. Daphne therefore found herself with the entire and considerable weight of the writer on her shoulders. He was incapable, she sobbed to her current lover, of blowing his own nose. She had to be on hand ten hours a day, buy his shaving cream, see to his laundry, fail to persuade him to pay his bills, engage and dismiss his charwomen, buy and send presents to his children and girl-friends, tell lies for him and occasionally even try to organise his murky, chilly soul. Leave, the lover advised her. But she felt needed.

She came wearing charcoal grey, her fairish hair hanging on either side of the lovely face like two damp flags at a funeral.

'Oho,' she said when she saw the blackboard. And then, 'When the hell is the ninth?'

'I don't know,' Eleanor said. 'Sometime next month.' She had been working hard all day, dragging, pulling, stretching, lifting, pounding more and more slowly up and down the now interminable stairs. Her shirt and rumpled jeans stuck to her body like old bandages. They sat in the kitchen, Daphne with the inevitable coffee, Eleanor with a warm whisky. Philip was downstairs doing some obscure electrical work of his own, having fixed all the plugs and fitted a dozen light bulbs.

'It's all very super,' Daphne said. 'Are you pleased?'

'Yes. Of course.'

'Has Dad seen it since you moved in?'

'No.'

'I bet,' Daphne said, fitting a tipped cigarette into a cancer-proof holder, 'that he'll be livid. He'll probably turn up soon, demanding to move in.'

'I doubt it,' Eleanor said.

Daphne shared, with deep distaste, her flat with a girl violinist. The flat was just round the corner, and Eleanor looked forward to the proximity. She always felt rather help-less with Daphne, whose troubles were of such vast propor-tions and whose passion for order almost exceeded her own.

'How's the job?' Eleanor asked, and looked at the black-board.

'Oh God . . . He was ill today, the last time he took his temperature it was ninety-eight point eight, dying. Some bird came round to open the champagne, thank God. I thought I was going to have to stay the night.'

'You mean he asked you to?'

'Of course. He can't sleep alone, he gets nervous. Have you heard from Cressida?'

'She sent a cable yesterday.'

'That can't come to any good—she can't possibly live in America, it'd kill her. And what about Jessie?'

'Still away. I haven't heard a word.'

43

'It's a bit much. She might send a postcard or something.'

So they droned on, complaining, questioning, answering, communicating like two members of a family who know each other so well, and so little, that conversation, consisting of sighs and groans and brief bursts of laughter, becomes almost wordless. This was how Eleanor and Mrs. Bennet used to talk, while Mr. Bennet mildly slumbered in the retreat that was called his study. But what had they talked about? Certainly not love or whether it was possible to go on living. Does she know what I've done? Eleanor wondered, does she really know? I hope she knows what she's done, Daphne thought, I hope she knows what she's up to.

'So I hope you're going to see that the old bastard gives you a great deal of money,' Daphne said. Mrs. Bennet grieved for the coarseness of her vocabulary, so unnecessary in such a pretty girl. Eleanor dimly recognised a kind of swagger, a rebellion against prettiness and niceness and ladylike subterfuge.

Nevertheless, she flinched at the question. In order to get money out of Graham, to demand her rights and payment for services given, she must be angry. She had not been angry for a very long time. Even waiting for him night after night, sorting out and folding up his lies and storing them away for future use, living through interminable weekends knowing that he was in Brighton or Paris (Graham was no pioneer) with some secretary or nurse or weedy starlet, she had not been angry. She had been, as it were, waterlogged with sadness, saturated in grief, the good, lively sense of anger had gone under. It was a kind of impotence. She tried, but couldn't feel it.

'I don't know,' she mumbled. 'I suppose there'll be some . . . arrangement.'

'Have you got a solicitor?'

'Yes,' she said humbly. 'Would you like some more coffee?'

'Is he any good? After all, Dad makes a fucking fortune conning people.'

'He's all right. It'll be all right. Would you like some more coffee?'

'Well, what are you living on?'

'I've got five hundred a year . . . you know, from my father. And I've saved a bit. Are you sure you wouldn't . . . ?'

'Five hundred a year! You must be joking! How the hell do you think you're going to keep up this house, and Philip, and everything else on five hundred a year!' Daphne, at any rate, could still get angry; the writer, who had yet to find it directed to himself, considered it one of her greatest assets. 'God Almighty, you're entitled to two-thirds of his income! You're not going to be stupid about this, are you?'

'No,' Eleanor said. 'And if I get broke I'll come to you.'

'Very funny,' Daphne said. 'You'd better try Cressida, all this flitting backwards and forwards across the Atlantic.'

'Or Marcus perhaps.'

'Oh, Marcus . . .' Daphne said, dismissing that idea.

.   .   .   .   .

By the end of the week Graham had bought a quantity of furniture that looked as though it had been designed for some psychedelic nursery, hired a gas cooker and moved back into the flat. His current secretary, a sturdy girl with cropped hair and ribbed tights, had helped him considerably; Nell Part-whistle had done absolutely nothing, but allowed herself to be moved without comment. The secretary, resenting the idle-ness of a girl younger than herself, burst into loud tears on Friday morning and gave notice. Two of Nell Partwhistle's school-friends moved in for the weekend, sleeping on mat-tresses on the floors of long empty rooms, hanging their hair pieces on picture nails like dead rabbits. There was a great deal of noise and activity. When he arrived home at midnight, early for once, they were all sitting on the floor drinking cocoa and painting their toenails. They hushed when he came in,

45

and the friends padded off to bed with carefully splayed toes, giggling a little when they thought they were out of earshot. Graham, who was shockingly tired, nevertheless felt serene and powerful. He had founded a patriarchy; he was in command; he had done, he thought once and for all, for Mrs. Bennet. Nell Partwhistle sat on his knee while he told her the events of the day. At the mention of so many famous names, she registered admiring interest. In fact she was rather bored, and looking tenderly down on the bald top of his head envied her school-friends their makeshift dormitory.

The next morning, Saturday, after he had cooked the breakfast and dressed himself with casual care, he determined to see Philip. Greatly to his relief, the boy answered the telephone.

'I'm sorry we couldn't have that supper the other evening, but I've been moving back into the flat. What about this evening?'

There was a long silence, then: 'Well . . . I'm awfully busy, actually.'

'What are you doing?'

'Well . . . I'm going back to school on Tuesday . . .' The voice trailed away, then suddenly growled, 'Why don't you come over here?'

'There? When?'

'I don't know . . .' Another silence. 'Mum says come for a drink about six.'

'No,' he said panicking. 'No, I can't. I have to see someone. I'll ring you later and we'll fix something. All right?'

But at half past five he told Nell Partwhistle, who was deeply indifferent, that he had to go and see a patient. Before he left he had to look up the address, which he had forgotten.

.   .   .   .   .

So that when he arrived, heavily armed with nonchalance, on the doorstep, he was unexpected. Philip was degutting his record player. Eleanor was on top of a step ladder. Daphne answered the door.

'My God,' she said. 'It's Dad.'

Surprised to see her, he fumbled for some adequate greeting. 'Hullo, lovely,' he said—she was, after all, a girl, though his daughter—and kissed her pallid cheek. 'How are you? How's everything?' He entered the house with his arm round her. For someone who had been brought up to behave well, she was not now sure how to behave. She led him towards the kitchen.

'Is Philip in?' he asked, noting his saucepans neatly on the shelves.

'I'll see . . .'

She ran upstairs to the sitting room. Eleanor was climbing the step-ladder with an armful of books.

'It's Dad,' Daphne said, in the tone of someone bringing catastrophe.

Eleanor felt a shock of happiness, swiftly followed by fear. 'But he said . . .' She stumbled down the ladder, dropped the books on the sofa. 'He said he couldn't . . .' She bit her knuckles, looking round the chaotic room. 'Where is he?'

'In the kitchen.'

'Is he angry?'

'I don't think so.'

She ran quickly down the stairs. He was wandering round the kitchen like a man at an art exhibition. At the moment he was studying the blackboard. She paused in the doorway, then said brightly, 'Hullo. I didn't think you could come.'

He turned and said, 'Hullo. I was just passing.' They avoided looking at each other. 'Nice place you've got here.'

'Yes. Would you like a drink?'

'What,' he asked, genuinely curious, 'have you got?'

'Everything except gin. But you don't drink gin.'

'Wine?'

'Of course.'

She went to her fridge and took out her wine and found

47

her corkscrew and gave him the bottle to open. He uncorked what he believed to be his wine with his familiar corkscrew and poured it into his glasses.

'Well,' he asked, 'how are you?'

She glanced at the blackboard. 'Fine. I'm fine. How are you?'

'Working too hard. Otherwise I'm fine.'

'You've moved back into the flat?'

'Yes. I had to spend a fortune on furniture.'

'Well,' she said lightly, 'one of us had to.'

'You might have warned me.'

'But you weren't living there, were you?'

The old impasse, weapons drawn, anger at the ready. Partly because he knew she was right (a quality in her he detested), and partly out of cowardice, he gave in. They had been together for a moment. Now his spirit walked away and left her alone. She ran after him quickly.

'If there's anything you want . . .'

'Well, if you had a couple of chairs to spare . . .'

'Of course.'

'No beds, I suppose?'

'No. Anyway . . .' She couldn't resist turning, when he thought all was peace, and pouncing again. 'I don't see that you need beds.'

'Well . . .' He thought of the school-friends, dossing down on the floor. 'Philip or Jessie might want to come and stay . . .'

She was at last brutally angry. He had invaded her home, her territory, and was now planning to plunder it. She got up abruptly and went to the door. 'If you think Philip or Jessie are going to go and stay with Nell Partwhistle, you're crazy.'

'Why not?' he asked blandly. 'She's perfectly harmless.'

She called for Philip, then went upstairs and sat on the sofa among the books. Murderous, her hands strangled each other; she stared down at them as though doing a victim to death. Now she could extort every last penny out of him, and a pound of flesh as well; now she could strip and expose him and send him limping off into some wilderness. At the same time she felt enormously unhappy, desolate inside her own rage. She told herself, as though talking to a child, that on the ninth she wouldn't care any more, all this would be over. The child inside herself considered this distant treat and rejected it. The child wanted love now, and to give love now, and to be with her proper parent, and to be reassured that no other child had taken her place. She wanted to be taken home; but this was her home.

Daphne came in and said awkwardly, 'Don't let the old bastard upset you.'

'No . . .' She released her hands, gave a kind of sob of laughter. 'No he doesn't . . . It's just that . . .'

'He shouldn't have come.'

'Well, I don't know . . . After all, why not? Is he talking to Philip?'

'They're standing about looking bloody miserable, if you can call that talking.'

'Damn, damn, damn . . . !'

Although the expletive was so mild, Daphne approved of it. She thought Eleanor was angry with Graham, and that it was about time. Eleanor was angry with God, particularly for not existing. She ran downstairs and caught them in the hall, looking shifty.

'Dad wants me to go back with him for supper,' Philip said.

'Oh yes?' She was quite ready to fight. Graham put his arm round Philip's shoulders. The two men stood looking at her. 'Do you want to?'

'Well . . . if it's all right . . .' He knew that she felt he was betraying her, and hated himself for her sense of betrayal.

'Of course it's all right,' Graham said. 'I'll bring him back.'

'Then why'—she actually heard herself laughing—'don't you go?'

She ushered them to the door, her departing guests. Graham put his arms round her for a moment, stiffly. She stood within his arms, her head awkward against his chest. 'Remember,' he said gently, 'I'm always there.'

She looked up at him with amazement. He was blessing her in the name of the father and the son: a benediction before he rose slowly through the April sky and took his place beside Nell Partwhistle in some unimaginable heaven. Perhaps he expected her to thank him for this act of grace. Perhaps she should kiss his hand.

'Always where?' she asked.

Irritated, as possible she had intended him to be, he took Philip's arm and hurried him down the steps and into the car. With a snarl and a roar the car streaked off down the quiet street. Daphne, standing alone at the window, turned as Eleanor came into the room.

'The old sod,' she said with great sadness. 'He didn't even say goodbye.'

6

Cressida Strathearn in Virginia lay in bed battling, between bouts of uneasy sleep, with the Bennets. The clapboard house where she had lived with her lover for six months was full of sunlight; it looked out on green lawns and neat paths, faculty wives with their litters of children packed into station wagons, the trees already heavy with leaves. The English girl, all blood drained from her face by the effort of rest, lay between candy-striped sheets, realised she should be up preparing lunch, heaved the blankets over her head with an enormous tug that left her feet stranded, white and thin and naked at the end of the bed.

Get up, child, her grandmother said, you can't lie here all day. Why not, Cressida asked. Put on your jeans and T-shirt if you must, her grandmother said, but there's ham and salad in the fridge, surely that's not too much to ask. Oh, much too much, Cressida said. Tom's a good man, Eleanor said, it's not his fault if he's got three children and a wife who won't divorce him. It is his fault, Cressida said, and I want a baby. But my dear child, Mrs. Bennet asked, without being married? Certainly, Cressida said. Then go ahead and have one, Eleanor said, setting, as usual, an impossibly high standard of courage. Oh bloody hell, Cressida said, and covered her face with the pillow and went to sleep for five minutes.

51

When she woke they were still there; they were always there. It's such a pity you're ruining your career, dear, said Mrs. Bennet, just when you were doing so well. I don't give a damn about my career, Cressida said, I want to have a baby. Yes, Eleanor said, I should like you to have a baby. Poor fellow, Graham said, making a brief appearance and vanishing again : give him a chance. Why don't you come home, Eleanor said, and think it over.

Go back, after all these years of independence, to Mother? She had let her flat and left her job to follow Tom to America. She loved him, almost old enough to be her father, lean and patient and obstinate in his cardigan and grey flannel trousers; his white head had seemed at first as tall as the sky. When they had lived in London, and were both working, it had been a perfect life. She had been quite certain that she couldn't live without him. What does that mean? Tom asked. You're a free human being, you must do exactly as you like. All right, Cressida said, I'll show him I can live without him and see how he likes that. She hurled herself out of bed and pulled on her jeans and T-shirt, then brushed her hair back severely and strapped it with a rubber band. There's a good girl, Mrs. Bennet said, you feel better now, don't you?

They sat in the kitchen among the unused machinery, Tom mildly eating ham and salad and drinking a glass of milk, Cressida chain-smoking over her coffee.

'What did you do this morning?' he asked hopefully, knowing the answer.

'Nothing.' She paused, letting him worry. 'I thought a bit.'

He was pleased, regarding thought as a perfectly adequate occupation.

'What did you think about?'

'What we were talking about last night, and the night before, and the night before that. Me, I suppose.'

'And did you reach any conclusion?' Careful, concerned, he might have been interviewing one of his students.

'No. Yes. I think I might go home for a bit.'

He took his pipe out of his pocket, packed it, lit it. 'Of course,' he said. 'If that's what you want to do . . .'

'You know what I want to do!' She controlled herself quickly. 'Shall I go?'

He smiled wanly and took her hand. 'My darling child, I can't tell you what to do. You're free.'

'I'm not free!' she shouted. 'I mean I don't want to be free! Why can't you tell me what to do? Why can't you tell me what you *want* me to do?'

'I want you to do what will make you happy.'

'Oh Christ,' she said, 'you know what would make me happy.'

'If you want a child, you must go ahead and have one. Of course.'

'But it's nothing to do with you?'

'No,' he said earnestly. 'It's nothing to do with me.'

'But if I got pregnant, here, now?'

'Then you would have to decide what to do.'

'Would you want me to get rid of it?'

'No. But you would have to do what you thought best.'

'Don't you,' she demanded, 'have *any* responsibility?'

He considered for a moment. 'No,' he said. 'I am not responsible. You must make up your mind.'

'I'll go, then.'

'Very well.'

She turned on him, ugly in tears. 'You don't care! You don't give a damn! You're probably glad to get rid of me!'

'I care very much,' he said, slightly roused, 'but I can't live your life for you.'

'Life!' she said, with dreadful scorn. 'What's that?'

'What you should be living.'

'And I could, couldn't I, if it weren't for your bloody wife and children . . .'

'We can't alter that.'

'But if we had a baby . . .'

53

'If you had a baby,' he corrected, 'it would alter your life. No doubt.'

They had said it all before. He was implacable. She hated him, but had committed herself to him. She loved him, but it was not enough. After these arguments she was reduced to a state of bewildered frustration which half killed her; she became, in fact, half dead, lying in bed all morning, not eating, her heart beating so slowly that it barely kept her alive. He would go back to his *Beowulf* and his students, who ran and jumped as though they had springs in their bodies, healthy girls with clear whites to their eyes, many of them virgins. Cressida felt old. At twenty-four she was looking for grey hairs, and her mouth sagged at the corners.

After he had gone she rang up the airline and booked her flight. Then she sent a cable to Eleanor announcing her arrival. It was lucky that Eleanor now had a house of her own, because she couldn't have gone back if Graham had been there, resenting her and treating her like a girl to be won over. Her father's sex life appalled her with its vulgarity. On the other hand, she was proud of Eleanor, and wanted her to have many lovers. She thought of Mrs. Bennet, of tea in the garden and confidences and hot-water bottles. She began to feel almost hopeful and packed her suitcases with unaccustomed energy, throwing away her contraceptive pills because she wouldn't need them at home.

.   .   .   .   .

Jessica had turned north and was travelling by lorry and Citroën and Mercedes, homewards. She had picked up an Irish boy with hair down to his shoulder blades and a gentle manner. His name was Brian, and he talked a great deal in his soft voice, telling her about Iraq and Turkey, and Morocco beyond the Atlas Mountains. They had slept side by side on beaches and in fields, but only occasionally made love. Jessica felt concern for his thin white body, hardly ever exposed to the sun; after he had smoked a couple of reefers he would lie on her large breasts as though on a cloud, smiling into her flesh. Neither of them knew each other's surnames. He left her in Paris. 'Goodbye,' they said. 'See you around.'

She had run out of money, and needed to wash her hair, so she arrived barefoot on Marcus's doorstep, noting with mild disgust the clipped bay trees and polished knocker. Marcus was working on a film script of the life of Kafka, an unhappy enterprise, and almost welcomed the interruption. He did not know what to do with her, or what to say to her, and feared for Marcel's onyx and gold bathroom; but she was his sister, and in principle he was fond of her. She lumbered in with her guitar and a large bunch of marigolds she had bought with her last franc. He took the marigolds, which in fact she had bought for herself, and put them in an art nouveau vase, where they looked ridiculous. He looked away from her blackened feet and gave her a mushroom omelette and a peach, and a glass of Chablis which she didn't drink.

'So Madam's moved out at last,' he said. 'Is she happy?'

'I don't know. I've been away. I should think she'll find it a bit funny, living on her own.'

'But you'll be there, won't you?'

'I suppose so . . . I don't know . . .'

'Why? Have you got plans?'

'Not really.' She took another peach, wiping her chin on the back of her hand as the juice ran down. 'I don't know . . .'

'You're a hard-hearted little miss,' he said acidly. 'You always were.'

'No,' she said. 'I'm not hard-hearted. It's just that I don't know.'

'But you wouldn't live with the father and that terrible doxy, would you?' he asked, shocked.

'I shouldn't think so,' she said, and gave him one of her rare smiles. 'I don't know.'

He packed her off to the bathroom, tempted to give her the

55

poodle's towels, but relented and loaded her with bath essence, shampoo, talcum powder, a bathrobe, nail scissors and toothpaste. She splashed about for a long time, and came out looking damp and rosy, with a grimy tidemark round her neck. He took her back into the bathroom and scrubbed her neck with a nail brush while she held up her hair, protesting. He lent her a pair of his own jeans, which strained over her woman's hips, and a pale blue cashmere sweater. When she had combed her wet hair she looked almost respectable. He suggested they went out for a drink, but she said she was tired and didn't drink anyway. He sat her down in front of the television, which she watched with pleasure and very little comprehension; the poodle, fascinated by her curious smell, lay across her knees with its head on her belly and shivered with rapture.

Marcus enjoyed looking after people. He slaved, as he often said, for Marcel. When he was halfway through making his daube, which had been marinating for two days in his orderly larder, Jessica mentioned that she didn't eat meat. He flew into a panic and drank most of a bottle of rosé to calm his nerves, then began to prepare a cheese soufflé. When Marcel came home, irritated and exhausted by the fact that his revolve had proved twelve centimetres too large for the stage and that an aluminium tree had fallen from the flies and hit a silly little girl on the head, Marcus was in no mood, as he put it, for chaff. Jessica listened curiously to their quarrelling, which, unlike most quarrelling, amused her because it didn't seem to be real.

'And on top of it all,' Marcel was hissing in the kitchen, 'we have this enormous girl looking like some refugee from under a stone and without shoes!'

'She happens to be my sister,' Marcus said with dignity. 'And if you don't like it, my dear, you can go, that's all, you can just go!'

'Then I shall go!' Marcel sat down in the rocking chair and rocked himself furiously. Marcus elaborately stepped over his feet to get to the cooker. Jessica appeared in the doorway looking benign.

'Can I do anything to help?' she asked. Both men looked at her despairingly. 'I'm quite happy,' she said, 'with baked beans.'

Order was at last restored. Jessica was allowed to lay the table and light the candles. As the evening went on, Marcel found her quite tolerable and Marcus became over-excited, dancing by himself among the red leather sofas and Grecian busts, beautiful and elegant and as queer, Jessica told herself sadly, as a bent kipper. At last Marcel, who was over fifty and overworked, went to bed with the poodle, and brother and sister were left together, half asleep.

'How's Philip? How has he taken it?'

'It's best, you know, for everyone,' she said sagely.

'But I'm worried about her.'

'Who?'

'Madam. It's not very jokey, being alone at her age. Somebody should be looking after her.'

She's not that old. Anyway, she's got a fellow. Some knight or other.'

'How do you know?'

'Daphne told me. She told Daphne.'

'Who is he? What does he do? Is it serious?'

'I don't know.'

'I think I ought to go over and take a look. I mean, now she's alone. Supposing she gets ill or something?' He was deeply distressed, his sense of impotence a physical discomfort.

'She's never ill. She's like Grandmother Bennet.'

'God, you're a tough little monster. What about Daphne? Is she helping a bit?'

'I don't know,' Jessica said, exasperated at last. 'I haven't been there.'

'How that bastard can go off and leave her now, at her age, is . . . Christ, it's beyond me. If he'd done it ten years ago . . .'

'I don't think you should talk like that,' Jessica said. 'I don't think you understand at all.'

'Why? Because I live over here? Because I'm queer? I understand a great deal, my child, and that's more than you seem to do. Your own mother.' He was almost in tears, intolerably enraged by what seemed to him her smug femininity, her implied loyalty to their father, whom he would like to murder, tear, shred, desecrate, demolish.

'I just don't think you understand,' Jessica said. 'That's all.'

She went to bed rather sadly in the small, rose-smothered guest room. Her family, she thought, was like this room: too comfortable, too hot and far too crowded. She remembered lying on the beach with Brian and the feeling she had had then of immense compassion and love for all living creatures, the fish and the children, the worms and the birds, the old men and women, and the little cows she had seen in a field. Why didn't this pity extend to her family? Why, except for Philip, didn't she love them? She folded Marcus's trousers and sweater and put her own ragged jeans and shirt ready to wear in the morning. He had given her a hundred francs, and she would start out early; by tomorrow evening she should be home, if the lifts were good. 'Home?' she asked herself; and went to sleep with the question, whatever it meant, unanswered.

.　　　.　　　.　　　.　　　.

Philip went back to school with a headful of confused impressions, a particularly sharp sense of parting, and considerable relief. When Eleanor, painfully curious, had asked him about his supper with Graham, he had mumbled that it was fine. He said nothing about Nell Partwhistle, whom he rather liked, or about the friends sleeping on the floor. He did blurt out that Graham had some smashing new furniture, which Eleanor took as a criticism of her taste for Victoriana and homeliness. Her paralysing respect for this son, and her awareness of the damage that could be done to him, kept her quiet. He might have preferred her to shout at him, or show some emotion other than persistent love.

Graham had decided that Philip's education was to be as different as possible from Marcus's. If he stayed at home he would be crushed by the Bennet women; he was sent, therefore to a progressive, co-educational boarding school where, in his curiously oblique way, he thrived. Ninety per cent of the children's parents were divorced or separated and he was quite pleased that he could now be considered normal. Most of his friends went to the station alone and he wished he could persuade Eleanor not to take him, but was too considerate of what he imagined her feelings to be.

'You don't have to wait,' he implored politely as they stood by the barrier in a crowd of young men and women loaded with haversacks and guitars.

She felt conspicuous. 'No. Well, then . . . I won't wait.'

'Write to me,' he said gruffly.

'Of course I'll write to you.' She was weeping behind her face, which was set in an expression of grim gaiety. 'And you write to me too.'

'I will.'

She kissed him briefly, conscious of the emancipated, elderly children who might despise him for it.

'I'll come and see you soon,' she said.

'Yes. All right.'

She stood back, pretending to leave, and he went through the barrier, guitared and haversacked like the rest, loping along like a boy who could walk twenty miles without tiring. As she watched, he was joined by a girl wearing a large hat and a serge cloak. He disappeared with her into the train, into his own life.

Her dread of his going away had led her into odd superstitions: each time, before they left for the station, she cleared away every possible trace of him, stripped his bed, washed up and put away every plate and mug, hid the chess and the Scrabble where they couldn't be seen when she returned home. Nothing, when she came back from saying goodbye to him, must remain to remind her. The thought that this time, for the first time, she was going back to an empty house both appalled and excited her. For the first time in twenty-six years she had absolutely nothing to do, except prepare for Kilcannon. She needn't cook a meal, she could lie in bed late, she could read, she could have her hair done when she liked, join a Health Club, telephone . . . She could learn about gardening, go for walks, need never watch television, she could telephone . . . Very slowly, although she always got stuck at the idea of telephoning, the elation took over from the sharp pain of parting from Philip. She was even singing inside her head, a little shocked by her own treachery. She would telephone . . . Alex, and they would go out to dinner.

When she drew up outside the house there was a small camp on the doorstep: Jessica, her guitar, two large paper bags and a puppy.

'I found her in Dover,' Jessica said. 'I hope you don't mind . . .'

'Mind?' She hugged her large, dirty daughter, wondering what they could have for supper. 'Of course I don't mind.'

'She's called Juniper,' Jessica said. 'I didn't have a key so I just waited.'

'I'll give you a key,' Eleanor said.

She opened the front door. A cable was lying on the mat. Juniper escaped from Jessica's arms and bounded on to the moss green stair carpet, where she peed liberally.

'Oh dear,' Jessica said lovingly. 'Juniper . . . don't.'

Eleanor said, 'Cressida's coming home.'

'That's nice,' Jessica said.

'Yes,' Eleanor said happily, relieved, diverted from danger. 'That's lovely.'

7

'The point is,' Cressida said, 'what do we do on Thursday?'

Jessica scooped up Juniper from inside the fridge and slammed the door shut. 'Why? What happens on Thursday?'

'It's the ninth,' Daphne said, prodding her cigarette in the direction of the blackboard. 'Can't you read?'

'Oh,' Jessica said. 'Well, why do we have to do anything?'

'You can't expect Mum to have a lovely romantic evening with us around,' Cressida said. 'We'd better go and stay with Grandmother Bennet.'

'We don't have to be out all night, do we?'

'I hope so,' Cressida said.

'Grandmother Bennet won't like Juniper.'

'If you will let her pee all over the place . . .'

'She's nervous, that's all. We'll go somewhere else.'

'Where will you go?'

'I don't know. Somewhere.'

'You can't come to me,' Daphne said. 'That bloody girl saws away all night. With any luck she's going to get married.'

'Well, I'll go somewhere,' Jessica said, feeling outcast.

'I'm going to Grandmother Bennet,' Cressida said, 'and you can do what you like.'

The small, attenuated house was now crowded. Jessica had taken some sort of possession of her room, where she refused to have carpet or curtains. It was a pretty room, looking down on the tops of trees. Jessica liked barns, attics, warehouses, caves, railway stations and the open air. She did not like pretty rooms.

With the help of cut-outs and Sellotape, strings of beads and old blankets, she managed to make it a little awkward, but it still cried out for white muslin and there was no space to dance or move. She put Juniper in a large carpet bag and went on the bus to see Graham, but that was just as unsatisfactory in its own way; Graham told too many jokes and Nell Partwhistle smiled too much, and, worst of all, they obviously disliked Juniper. At least Eleanor kept quiet about her ruined carpets, seeming to realise that life was more important than Wilton. In fact Eleanor was outraged, but hadn't the courage to say so. She deeply wanted Jessica to feel at home, and to be happy, so pretended to put up with the old bones and chewed socks and turds on every landing. Jessica, who had no idea how to train the puppy, and didn't believe in training anyway, tried to clear up for Eleanor's sake, but the task was Augean and she became worried.

Cressida slept in Philip's room, a visitor. She did not try to imprint her personality on it, but hung her dresses on an expandable clothes horse and kept her beads and rings and chains in a soup bowl. She felt she ought to get a job and telephoned a couple of art directors who had employed her in the past. 'Darling,' they both said, 'we all thought you'd emigrated. There's not a scrap of work, why not try commercials?' Tomorrow, next week, sometime, she would try commercials; but the idea of dressing sets for washing powder or cat food did not appeal to her, and she had £200 in the bank, so why, immediately, bother? Out of guilt, she asked Eleanor to wake her every morning; otherwise she would have slept blissfully protected for most of each day. It was as though in her life she had come up against a bank of fog which she could not penetrate: until she could have a child, and find some function for her body, she was paralysed. She wrote long, loving letters to Tom, which he answered with measured affection. He missed her very much, and hoped that she was sorting things out.

Now Cressida was back, Daphne came more often. The kitchen became a conference room where the women sat round the table with their lists and pencils and address books and coffee and handbags, discussing the one who might be absent, complaining, gossiping, occasionally blurting out what they thought, at the moment, their real feelings to be. It was, during this time, a Bennet stronghold. The men in their lives, future suitors and old enemies, were outside the walls. The first one to be let in, an inaugural ceremony for the future, would be Patrick Kilcannon.

. . . . .

The house, or as much as he need see of it, was ready. It was a woman's house and the colours were those of fruit: orange, lime, avocado and lemon growing out of rosewood and dull mahogany. Some of it, like the rather pompous dining room, was a private joke: Eleanor had deliberately created a room for silver tureens and kippers and kedgeree, the reading of the *Morning Post* and the saying of grace, none of which would happen. Her bedroom, she said, was the same sort of joke: bridal, drapes and covers of white lace which before long would become grey and ragged round the edges. Now, however, it was crisp as a wedding cake and curiously unseductive. She felt uneasily that she had made a mistake somewhere, gone after the wrong image. But what was her image? A woman with large grey eyes and hair streaked like a cat, a smiling mouth that held bitterness, a huge soul crammed anyhow into a head that was too small to contain it. Her body, perhaps because she had never considered it very much, was young, as though it had never really noticed having children or the passing of so many years. She tended to move carelessly, as though there were some lack of co-ordination

63

between her will and her limbs; when she was a child this was known as clumsiness, she was continually dropping china and falling downstairs and her knees were always covered in scabs and bruises. She had in her life bought many hats, but never worn them; she owned no jewellery; some of her clothes, the ones she disliked, were high fashion, but mainly she dressed from chain stores and on the spur of the moment. Her rebellious spirit was like the small, steady pilot light of a great furnace which had never, by God or man or circumstance, been turned on. What was her image? It was not in any case the chaste fussiness of the room she had designed for her first night with Kilcannon.

On the eighth she told them that they must get their own food: Jessica made an elaborate vegetable stew, which she shared with Juniper, and Cressida did not eat. Eleanor prepared, for the first time in years, to cook for love. She worked quietly and carefully, tasting from time to time with her eyes shut, as though willing herself inside his mouth. By late afternoon the dishes and saucepans were set out, covered and ready for tomorrow's use. Although she would have liked to spend the evening going round the house looking at it, she went to the pictures with Daphne and Cressida. They thought she should have her mind taken off it. The film, which had something to do with some sort of unrecognisable love, did not take her mind off it. She sat in the dark smiling, her cheek in her hand, her eyes looking attentively at the screen, awake and dreaming.

On the ninth it was raining, hard, summer rain that blurred the windows of the high house and gave the feeling of being lost at sea. She let Juniper out of Jessica's bedroom and put the puppy out into the rain, where it ran about in the mud, whining pitifully. She brought it into the kitchen where it immediately and gratefully emptied its bladder. In her dressing gown, mopping up the mud and the mess, Eleanor thought this isn't the image either. Sometime during the day, when she was alone, she would find the right one.

Cressida borrowed Daphne's car and hissed off, windscreen wipers flailing, to Mrs. Bennet. The girl who came in to clean, an Irish child with three babies under five and a hostile husband, set to polishing: she had never lived in a house in her life and was baffled by the arrangement of stairs and corridors and landings which appeared perfectly useless but had to be cleaned. Her eldest daughter, in neat hair ribbons and shiny little plastic shoes, tottered laboriously up and down carrying dusters and gifts for Juniper. Eleanor went to the hairdresser, which she did very rarely and with the greatest reluctance. The day was organised in every detail, and everything must be perfect. She bought an armful of flowers and went back to decorate her house for its opening night.

Jessica had gone, leaving a note which said 'See you tomorrow'. Eleanor felt momentarily sad, guilty and absurd. The house loomed over her, silent, drowned in rain. They had gone out of concern for her, but wouldn't it have been better if he came to find them there, her people, her real self? With a sudden sinking of spirit, which soon revived, she told herself that Graham had no such problems; they were all expected to accept Nell Partwhistle, in bed or out. Kilcannon, however, was not Nell Partwhistle, but a man to be reckoned with. A new rush of love and delight swept her with flowers to every corner of the house; when they were done she turned on the radio and started polishing all the glasses, squinting at them against the light, sometimes singing a few words of the songs she knew.

It was about five o'clock when she realised that she hadn't got a suitable tray to put the drinks on. By suitable she meant a tray that wasn't either plastic or tin or chipped or inlaid with old egg. She hurried into the car and drove to the nearest department store where she bought a suitable, and expensive, tray. Coming out of the shop, she paused in the electrical department. Graham's record player had not been among her spoils, but she had brought her own records. Shouldn't they have music? Wasn't music, in fact, an absolute necessity?

She approached a small, elegant record player with caution, as though not wishing it to know that she had noticed it. A cunning assistant sold it to her in five minutes. She left the shop having spent £40, deeply hoping that he liked Vivaldi.

By seven o'clock the drinks were on the suitable tray, the ice bucket ready, the record player fluting Vivaldi, the table laid with the polished glasses and green candles, the food simmering and chilling at just the right temperatures. She went upstairs to get ready, preparing herself with the most intense concentration down to the last fingernail and eyelash. He must not be disappointed in her. She was beginning to feel frightened, even reluctant. The waiting had been so long; she had shut the thought of everyone else, even Graham, out of her mind, and now wondered for the first time whether she had been relying too much on the idea of a man whom, truthfully, she hardly remembered. She was aware that her surface feelings were entirely childish, charmed, part of a fairy-tale, growing, like all fairy-tales, from some grim and realistic need; but below this there was a genuine curiosity and concern for a man with whom for some reason of circumstance or chemistry or fate, she felt most deeply involved. She must not be disappointed in him. He was too important.

Perfumed, polished, moderately satisfied with herself, the bedroom looking as welcoming as possible, she went downstairs. The rain had stopped, the evening was liquid and golden. The high first-floor windows of the sitting room looked down on the street, and for a while she watched the cars going home, listening intently, and with some dread, for the diesel throb of a taxi coming round the corner. Then, playing a game, she decided to pretend that she wasn't waiting, poured herself a drink, substituted Barbra Streisand for Vivaldi and sat down in an armchair far from the window. Would they kiss when he arrived? What would they talk about? She smoked too much, dirtying the gleaming ashtrays.

At half past eight she went back to the window. There were fewer cars and the people in the neo-Georgian mansion opposite had turned on their silk-shaded lamps. A couple of empty taxis went by and an old man with long white hair on a bicycle. There was a miraculous sunset over Kilburn and when the street lights came on they looked at first too weak to be useful. She heard very clearly the time signal for nine o'clock from her neighbour's radio.

Alex had told her that she must have an Answering Service if she wanted to keep in touch. There was nothing more off-putting, he said, than people who were inaccessible. She forgot about it most of the time, but now she realised that Kilcannon must have telephoned while she was out and that there would be a message waiting. She telephoned the service and gave her number. There was a long pause, then the brisk voice said cheerfully, 'Nothing for you, Mrs. Strathearn.' She put the receiver down and sat in the dark, still waiting.

At half past ten she telephoned Cressida.

'What are you doing?' Cressida asked sharply. 'What's happened?'

She tried to control her voice, to sound indifferent. 'He didn't turn up.'

'You mean he just didn't turn up? Didn't phone or anything?'

'No.'

'What a *bloody* swine. How perfectly awful for you.

'It's all right. It doesn't matter. It was all very stupid anyway.'

'Perhaps his plane got held up or something.'

'Yes. Perhaps. Anyway, good night. I'll see you tomorrow.'

She went downstairs and turned the oven off. The celebratory dining table looked foolish, cheap, like an advertisement. She went very slowly up the stairs to bed, turning off the lights one by one. Her bedroom sneered at her. She lay down fully clothed on the white lace bed cover and tried to summon Mrs. Bennet to her rescue. It was very bad manners, child, you should be extremely angry. But I can't be angry, I can't. Mrs. Bennet was useless to her, as in her dreams, because what she wanted was a body beside her own, inside her own. Since Graham stopped touching me, she thought, I have become untouchable, a leper. 'When we are separated we will have a huge affair.' She dreamt that Graham was tasting her careful food and saying that it made him feel sick.

8

Mrs. Strathearn lived alone with her Siamese cat in an Edwardian apartment block behind the Albert Hall. She had lived there for thirty years, and regarded it as her manor. Where Mrs. Bennet went in for weaves and linen or even, at a pinch, hessian, Mrs. Strathearn never contemplated anything but brocade and, in the kitchen, gingham. She had accumulated an extraordinary assortment of china ornaments, which she dusted sometimes in the evening while watching television. There were many traces of her schoolmaster husband, prints and water-colours from Florence, Delphi, Pompeii and Paestum, and a few figurines from Crete which she still believed were the real thing. When the grandchildren were young they had found this profusion of little objects fascinating, but since they had not been allowed to touch them they had lost interest. Mrs. Bennet may have taught them to behave well; Mrs. Strathearn expected them to behave well. She was positively afraid of Jessica, who once—and once only—had brought that dreadful puppy to tea. A few days ago Jessica had rung her up and asked whether she could stay the night. 'Oh, no,' she had said, laughing with fear, 'I don't think so.' She had no idea how much, at the moment, Jessica longed for her father's mother.

Graham, after twenty-six years of guilty indifference, had taken his mother up again. She was delighted, not so much because she felt needed, but because it was so pleasant after thirty years of widowhood to feel loved. She went to the theatre with Nell Partwhistle, and if Graham didn't turn up they philosophically put their coats on his empty seat and agreed, with shared awe, that he was a busy man. There had been an uneasy hint of equality about Eleanor, a submerged violence and lack of respect. Mother and mistress were very happy, doting on their means of support and entirely uncompetitive. Graham basked in their approval, and if he occasionally felt a twinge of boredom attributed it to his liver.

One fine morning, after a day of torrential rain, Eleanor rang up and asked Mrs. Strathearn to lunch.

'Lunch?' Mrs. Strathearn asked, as though it were some ceremony she had never heard of.

'Yes,' Eleanor said. 'Today. Do come.'

'Well . . . at your house?'

'Yes,' Eleanor said. 'I'm at home.'

'Very well, then,' Mrs. Strathearn said, and she was so surprised that she added, 'Thank you.'

She dressed carefully, in matching tones of lavender, and took a hired car. The house, from the outside, was rather impressive. Poor Graham, she thought, what a dreadful responsibility. She rang the front doorbell and when Eleanor opened the door—dressed anyhow, as usual, and looking deadfully tired—her delicate nose was immediately assaulted by the most appalling smell of liquor.

'I'm sorry about the smell,' Eleanor said. 'I was carrying a tray of drinks downstairs, and I fell. It was all smashed. A new bottle of whisky.'

'Never mind,' Mrs. Strahearn said coldly. What was Eleanor doing with a tray of drinks upstairs, anyway? She had always suspected that Eleanor was, at heart, a libertine. 'I daresay if you open the windows . . .'

There were flowers everywhere: what extravagance. She sat neatly and nervously on a luxurious sofa and accepted a glass of sherry. She asked after the children: Cressida was

70

staying with Mrs. Bennet, Jessica was away, they would be coming back this afternoon.

'So you're here all alone?' Mrs. Strathearn asked, casting an eye from bedroom to basement.

'Yes,' Eleanor said. 'At the moment I am.'

Mrs. Strathearn was not a hard or malicious woman; she was in fact rather cowardly and nervous. Eleanor had always alarmed her a little with her tactless regard for truth and her ruthless dedication to some kinds of honesty. She had always admired her daughter-in-law, but had never felt sorry for her, and was not going to start now. She thought the house was extremely attractive, but was not going to say so, because Graham lived with all that dreadful pop furniture, which she deplored, and somehow it was Eleanor's fault. She was confused and overwhelmed, and wished she hadn't come.

The lunch confused her even more. Chilled watercress soup was followed by a casserole in which her sharp tongue detected thyme, rosemary, garlic, orange and lemon, tomato and a touch too much wine. Was this Eleanor's weekday lunch? The cheeses were fresh, the salad sweet and crisp; there were eleven bottles of wine in the wine rack, and new candles in the silver candlesticks. Mrs. Strathearn did not know whether to feel flattered, or angry on Graham's behalf.

Eleanor told her about Daphne's work, and Cressida's love affair, and Jessica's holiday, and as much about Philip as she could imagine. They hardly mentioned Graham, and did not once refer to Nell Partwhistle. Over their coffee, when Mrs. Strathearn had almost relaxed, Eleanor said, 'I'm glad you came. I don't see why, because I'm separated from Graham, I should be separated from you.'

Mrs. Strathearn, flinching away from a direct emotion, was nevertheless moved. 'It was very nice, dear,' she said. 'A delicious lunch, and I did enjoy hearing about the children.'

'I hope you'll come again,' Eleanor said, conscious of the old lady's sense of disloyalty.

'Tell the children they're always welcome,' Mrs. Strathearn

said. 'But not, please, that dreadful little dog.'

So the meal, which had been the food of love, had been eaten by her mother-in-law, and she had survived the day. In the afternoon she wrote a note to Kilcannon at his club: 'What happened? Please let me know, because I worry.' The wording was wrong—'worry' created a frowning and dour impression—but she posted it, and was reluctant to return to the house. She walked for a while in the bland and sunny streets, looking into people's front windows and trying to make out how they lived. Some kind of love, or at least obligation, was framed inside the oblongs of glass. Contemporaries lived together without too much resentment or fear. She had suffered from loneliness all her life, even when the children were young, and most of all with Graham; now, aimlessly wandering in the warm afternoon, she felt for the first time that it could become a sickness. Kilcannon had failed her and it must, in some obscure way, be her fault. Graham had left her: that must also be her fault. Anger would have been an antidote to this poison, but she could only feel it in brief, spasmodic outbursts; somewhere inside her, anger was being diverted and changed, by abominable alchemy, into grief. She only understood that after the excited anticipation of the last few weeks, she had a heavy heart. She did not know that she was becoming ill, and that the disease could prove fatal.

However, there was a lot of Bennet in her that was still uncorrupted. She told Cressida and Daphne the story of the previous evening and, by the art of dishonesty, made them laugh in spite of their horror. 'And then this morning, believe it or not, I was carrying this bloody tray downstairs and, I don't know, I slipped or something and there was the whole lot smashed. All over the place.'

'What did you do?' they asked, agog.

'I sat on the stairs and roared with laughter.' It was true, except that she hadn't roared, she had laughed almost silently, behind covering hands.

'And then what?'

72

'I don't know . . . it was a lovely morning. I went out into the garden . . .'

'Well,' Cressida said. 'So much for our Gaelic knight, the bastard.'

So much for him: far too much. She had stayed for nearly a month in the house, a month of the enormous future eaten away. Now she began to realise that this was not a visit, with an end that she could chalk on a blackboard; she was not a five-year-old child playing houses, able to move on when it was finished. This was where she lived, and might live for ever. She must stop waiting, anticipating; she must make sense of each hour as it passed. With Cressida and Jessica at home, she could persuade herself that she had certain duties to perform. It was not true, but Cressida and Jessica allowed her to believe it, eating their regular meals with relish and trying, for Eleanor's sake, to remember that the days should be arranged in some kind of order. They both found this hard. Jessica could only eat when she was hungry, which was usually about five-thirty in the evening, and Cressida came alive, like a cat, about midnight. During this time their true concern for their mother subdued them. Only Juniper was anarchic and indifferent.

Forcing herself to survey her life without Kilcannon, whom she thought had been a mirage, vanishing at arm's length, Eleanor returned to the realities of Alex and Ellis, whom she had almost forgotten. Buttressed by them, her friends and semi-lovers, she might venture further into the small scattering of acquaintances that had sparsely peopled her life with Graham. They were, when she tried to remember them, faceless and anonymous but they were neatly written down in her address book, Wymans and Ridgeways and Stephens and Macmillans, and they must exist somewhere. They were all couples, and Alex the only unattached man she knew. She telephoned him early one morning, to avoid speaking to him at the office.

Alex had loved Eleanor with all the passion, tenderness and concern that he could muster out of the heart he thought he knew. Since his analysis, some ten years ago, he also thought he knew the limitations of this heart, and apart from Eleanor had fed it mainly on infatuations for cheeky girls who thought him a perfect darling. His affair with Eleanor had seemed to him momentous; for a short time he had even thought of taking her over, Bennets and all, and of proving himself a stronger man (as, in some ways, he was) than Graham. But Eleanor, with her precarious hold on reality, her preoccupations, her alien spirit and her inner confusions, had proved too much for him. Baffled and wounded, he had comforted himself in the loving arms of a worldly and talented woman barrister, recently divorced. She had no children, and although her past might have provided material for a successful autobiography, it did not intrude on her sincere and grateful passion for Alex. Her name was Georgina, which inevitably became abbreviated to George: unsuitably, since she was aggressively feminine and looked, in court, as though she were playing Portia.

Eleanor knew little of this. It had not occurred to her that somebody else's life, after coming into close contact with her own, might rebound a million miles away, or shatter into little pieces and re-form itself into something unrecognisable. Alex had loved her, but she had not been available; Alex, of course, still loved her, and would come now he was needed. She believed Georgina to be a suitable friend for him, but did not consider that anything could destroy a devotion which, he had said, was unique in his life. What seemed, in retrospect, extreme selfishness and egoism on her part was simply ignorance. Other people's feelings, when expressed, or their development, when suddenly revealed, amazed and often shattered her. Is that what they've been feeling? Is that what they've been doing? Why wasn't I told, why didn't I know? Because, my dear—they might have said, but didn't— you were too busy pointlessly trying to clear up that junk shop inside your head; the windows are boarded over, and other people's seasons come and go unheeded.

Alex and Georgina were in bed when the telephone rang.

'Let it ring,' Alex said, secure in his Answering Service.

'No,' Georgina said. 'It might be somebody in trouble. It might be Eleanor.'

He picked up the receiver and barked into it, 'Hullo.'

Eleanor didn't think it necessary to announce her name. 'How are you? I haven't seen you for ages.'

'I'm fine, fine.' He mouthed 'Eleanor' to Georgina, who tactfully got out of bed and padded, naked, to the bathroom. 'How are *you*?'

'Well . . . all right. I'd like to see you.'

'Yes. Of course. When?'

'Well . . . I don't know . . . What are you doing this evening?'

'Sorry. I've got to go to a party at Annie Broch's.'

A tremendous effort was being made on the other end of the line. He was half aware of it, and dreaded it. The cheerful voice said, 'Couldn't I come too?'

'I don't think it's really your cup of tea, darling. Let's make it lunch on . . .'—he was never without his diary, even putting it within reach of the lavatory during his morning sessions—'let me see . . . Wednesday.'

There was a long pause. He said, 'Hullo? Are you still there?'

'Yes. Wednesday, then. Where?'

'I'll call you in the morning, when I know where I'm going to be. All right?'

'Yes. All right.'

'See you on Wednesday, then. Take care.'

Georgina came back and sat on the edge of the bed, wearing his dressing gown.

'How is she?'

'Oh, she sounds all right.'

'I worry about her rather. I mean . . . I've rather buggered things up for her, haven't I?'

'No,' he said, taking her firm hand. 'You haven't buggered anything up. You're wonderful.'

She smiled the smile that judges and magistrates found distracting.

'You know, I think you mean that.'

'With all my heart.'

She lay beside him, opening the dressing gown, preparing to bury him in kisses as though in sand. Physically, she adored him. When he thought of his love-making with Eleanor—which he did more and more infrequently—it was as something savage, electric, unpredictable and curiously unshared. He basked in Georgina's amorousness, which administered to him and prised open his heart, a gentle and persuasive seducer. They were both middle-aged and both, with a kind of mutual awe and light-heartedness, had found happiness. Their shared world had become so small that it fitted like a sweet globe inside their meeting, open mouths.

. . . . .

Eleanor would hardly admit to it, even to herself, but she was reluctant to leave Cressida and Jessica during the day. They were safe in their sunny house, eating their scrappy food, not venturing into the indifferent city. Going out to lunch meant getting dressed, making up her face, altering her handbag, driving south into foreign parts. It also meant dealing with the afternoon when the food and the wine and the brandy were finished. Cressida, still in her dressing gown and reading for the fifth time a letter from Virginia, applauded her mother's appearance.

'You're daft,' she said. 'The way I feel this morning, you look young enough to be my daughter.'

'Why not take Juniper on the Heath?'

76

'Because I've got a million things to do, and Jessica can bloody well take Juniper on the Heath.'

'What have you got to do?'

'Do my washing, go to the cleaners, take my shoes to be mended . . .' Her voice trailed away at the immensity of her tasks.

Eleanor hung about. 'I wish I didn't have to go.'

'Oh, go on,' Cressida said, exasperated. 'Have a good time. And tell Alex to pull his finger out.'

Eleanor had never known what this odd phrase meant, but she realised that Cressida was still match-making, trying to hustle her into some interesting intrigue. She backed the car out of the garage and paused to let a girl cross the pavement. The girl, not realising that Eleanor was waiting, also paused. The girl had smudged black eyes, dank hair and a PVC raincoat, in spite of the weather. Eleanor, turning in her seat, waved her on. The girl raised a limp hand and plodded behind the back of the car. As she backed into the street Eleanor saw her crossing the road towards a dismal and forbidding pub where she had once, on a desperate Sunday, bought a bottle of Spanish Sauternes like a symptom of jaundice.

Alex had chosen the usual restaurant, within walking distance of his office. It took Eleanor three-quarters of an hour to get there, and then she parked on a yellow line under a traffic warden's indignant eye. The lunch, therefore, had already cost her two pounds. She was well known—they had eaten most of their meals here in the days when they held hands between courses—and the head waiter greeted her effusively, leading her down the stairs into the glass-walled greenhouse where stocky lads from Cyprus, Norwich and the Isle of Wight played at being Italian waiters. '*Bon giorno, signora . . . Com 'esta?*' Teeth flashed, serviettes beat back and forth like fly-whisks, the already impeccable table was rearranged with lightning speed, the boys in their striped vests stood panting as though ready to dash off into the undergrowth for a doggy ball. 'An aperitif, signora? Campari soda? *Va bene*. Luigi, campari soda!'; and the huge menus were produced like a conjuring trick, her cigarette was lit by an Olympic flame that had been running at high speed from Santa Lucia, hysteria was a rampant covering for their weary, flat-footed and underpaid souls.

'Well,' Alex said, when it was all over. 'And how's tricks?' He often used phrases out of his childhood reading. He had even been known to say 'Hi, gang'.

Eleanor had determined, on the way down, to talk to him, to get it straight. Here am I, she had been going to say, alone; and where are you? Or something of the sort. Now all she said, smiling with her eyes, was, 'All right. How are your tricks?'

'Fine. Fine.' He, too, had determined to tell her about Georgina. But she was looking exceptionally pretty, even fragile, and he felt temporarily engulfed in a pleasurable nostalgia. 'Skinny,' he said, touching her cheek with the back of his hand. 'You need feeding up a bit.'

'It's all those stairs.'

'But you're happy there,' he stated. 'Happier.'

'Oh, yes, happier,' she said, correctly returning the ball to the right part of the court.

'And how are the girls?'

She considered for a moment telling him about Cressida, her anxiety for Cressida. But it was not part of this particular game. She said that they were all fine—the word that encompassed everything from bounding health to the near-death of a stick insect—and amused him with Daphne's horrific life with the writer, and Jessica's devotion to Juniper; and finally, as the campari flowed stickily down her throat, she made up a story about a woman who had prepared for two days for a man to come to dinner, and how the woman had waited, and how, would you believe it, he had never turned up. It was a good story.

78

'What a bastard, though,' Alex said, patting her hand. 'Poor baby.'

'Oh, no,' she said, and actually giggled, looking down into the pink dregs. 'It was rather funny, really. Perhaps he doesn't even exist.'

He knew, without wanting to know, that something was wrong with her. For instance, that was a puzzling, unnecessary thing to say. Perhaps she might begin to reveal herself, a terrible, unwieldy lump of unhappiness. In which case, what could he do? He was powerless, and could only hurt her further. He must at all costs avoid anything approaching the truth. Expertly, he changed course, sped off into familiar waters. He had been to the theatre, seen a couple of films, Annie Broch's party had been a drag 'but we managed to leave early'.

Her eyes flickered upwards, enquiring, questioning the 'we'.

'Georgina came with me,' he said stiffly. 'You know. Georgina Bronhurst.'

'Oh yes,' she said. 'Georgina.'

He knew Eleanor well enough to know that all was now discovered. She might be extraordinarily obtuse over some things, the mathematics of life, the inevitability of cause and effect, the impossibility of fitting square pegs into round holes; but the mere mention of that one word, which described two people as being a whole, had revealed to her every detail, every intricacy of the relationship between himself and Georgina. He felt appallingly guilty, and deeply relieved.

'So how is it,' she asked carefully, 'with you and Georgina?'

'Very good. Emotionally, mentally . . . sexually. Very good.'

'I see.' She put her knife and fork together with as much neatness as a well-brought-up child. 'That's . . . splendid.'

The game was over. He took her hand. 'You don't have to say it's splendid.'

'But it is. I'm very glad. Will you . . . get married?'

'I shouldn't think so. Why should we?'

79

'I don't know.' She laughed politely. Mrs. Bennet was delicately cheering her on, willing her to victory, sitting firmly on the boxed-in confusion that threatened to erupt through the top of her head. 'Why shouldn't you?'

'There doesn't seem any point.'

She drank some wine, acid white, that made her mouth squirm at the corners. 'Will you . . . do you live together?'

'More or less.' It was only his concern for her, the residue of love, that made him go on with this conversation. 'I'm thinking of buying a house in the country.'

'You?' She meant you the classic bachelor with your two-roomed flat, every meal eaten in restaurants, a char who acts as nanny; you who are always sleeping when your women steal away with their underclothes stuffed in their handbags, sometimes leaving notes on the memo pad to say goodbye. 'A house?'

'We might. Will you come and stay?'

'But Georgina . . .'

'My friends will come and stay,' he said, 'and you are my friend.'

When she got home both Cressida and Jessica were out. She sat in her town clothes at half past three in the afternoon. There are things to be done, she told herself. What things? And what for? A silly jingle kept going through her head: I care for nobody, no not I, and nobody cares for me. The song was meant to be merry: carefree. There was a jolly miller once lived on the River Dee . . . What made him jolly, his wife, children, work, or just the blessing of carelessness? Her mind, as she lay in an armchair, her arms loose by her sides, was briefly occupied by this miller, whom she saw as in an illustration to a child's rhyme, fat and floury, with a chef's hat on his head and a grinning, rubicund face. And nobody, he sang, with the greatest satisfaction, cares for me. She stretched out a limp arm for the telephone, intending to ring Mrs. Bennet, who would at least be talkative. Instead, she dialled Ellis's number.

'Ellis Cromer,' the voice growled. She knew at once that he was slightly drunk.

'It's me.' She tried an entirely new approach, unconsciously evolved in the last few moments. 'I want to talk to someone.'

There was a huh of laughter. 'Well, then, talk away.'

'Can't you come round?'

'Now?'

'Whenever you like.'

'I can't, love. Gwen's going off to Russia, of all places, tomorrow on one of these student-exchange things. Of course, they won't let her in if they know she's associated with your Cromer. But you know how it is, I feel I ought to stick around . . .'

'Yes, of course.' Bitchily, guiltily, her heart had lightened. 'How long is she going for?'

'About five weeks. Of course, nobody cares what happens to me.'

'Oh, yes,' she said. 'I do.'

'Well, you're about the only one. I'll come round tomorrow night and sob on your shoulder.'

'All right,' she said. 'Do that.'

'Was there anything special'—he sounded wary—'you wanted to talk about?'

'No.'

'You're sure, because'—a grunt of laughter—'I'm all ears. Big, hairy ones, stickin' out all over.'

'Bless you,' she said. 'See you tomorrow.'

She had no sexual what Mrs. Bennet would have called designs on Ellis; or, indeed, on Alex. Sexually, she was in reality aching for the inaccessible Graham; in fantasy, longing still for the intangible Kilcannon. Even more sharp than her need for sex, at the moment, was the need to have someone at her side, accompanying her out into the world, someone who would be part of that absolutely necessary 'we'. She was sure that Ellis, without Gwen, would feel the same need. A couple thrown together by circumstances, they could plunder the trinkets of London: go to the Zoo (they used to do that, in the old days), walk in the park, go to art exhibitions (he would hate that), the movies, junk shops, drink beer on the bank of the sludgy Thames. If he was working, she would sit quiet in the studio, ready with the scotch that Gwen denied him. And if they became lovers again, more by mistake than anything else, she would enjoy his heavy, probably snoring, weight beside her, and relinquish him quite happily to Gwen on her return.

Comforted, she went downstairs to make some tea. A letter, which must have come by the second post, had been left on the hall table. She carried it, her thumb over the Irish postage stamp, into the kitchen and switched on the kettle. She looked at the envelope back and front. The water boiled, she made the tea, placing tea, pot, milk, cup and saucer on the suitable tray. She waited patiently for the tea to brew, then poured it out and lit a cigarette.

'No,' the letter began, with no introduction, 'you must not be worried, although it is very kind. The story is simple and frustrating. I had a telegram which required me to be in Dublin at 6.30 on Thursday, which meant a flight there from Shannon and no possible way of getting in touch. One of the lunatic things about my life is that I am seldom alone and yet there is no one I can trust to do all the simple things like sending telegrams and making telephone calls.'

'Tomorrow I go to the States and Canada for three weeks, visiting needy relatives and fixing up some business there—I shall be in London on May 28th. If you feel like taking the obvious risk it would be nice if you would keep the evening of June 1st free. Patrick.'

Risk? Every nerve jumped at the word. What risk? And why obvious? She felt none of her original elation. With a kind of self-ridicule she went to the blackboard, wiped it clean of tomato ketchup, flour and spaghetti, and wrote 'Patrick June 1st' and added a small, beautifully executed question mark.

9

Jessica had found herself a job helping in a children's playground in West London. She was paid £5 a week, and Juniper was her invaluable assistant. She did not regard the job as something she did at regular hours for a small amount of money: it became a way of life. In the tottering squares of Notting Dale and Ladbroke Grove she felt more at home than since, as a small child, she had learned what a home was meant to be. Together with a young Jamaican and a drop-out from the London Polytechnic, both of whom the police regarded with suspicion, she created a lively anarchy in the playground, was dragged by the children into their homes where she sat on the floor making black dolls out of old stockings, puzzles from pebbles, paintings with tomato sauce and soot. One day she saw Brian loping along on the other side of the wire netting that fenced the playground. She ran to him, radiant with pleasure, and pulled him into the mob, where at first he was uneasy. The children swarmed over him, rifled his haversack, tugged at the crucifix on his thin chest. They asked him a hundred questions in accents he couldn't understand. One small girl in a dimity white dress and ribbons in her corkscrewed hair gave him a tin ring which fitted, since his hands were small, on his little finger. He smiled over their heads at Jessica. That night they spent together in the Jamaican's room with Juniper sleeping between their feet.

That night, also, Ellis stumbled, swerved like a rudderless galleon, groped and lurched his way to Eleanor's house. He had been drinking all day, in fury at Gwen's desertion. Sometime this afternoon, he dimly realised, he should have taken her to the airport. 'Let her find her own fucking way to the airport,' he mumbled to some gatepost he had been passing at the time. He didn't know whether he had eaten anything during the day, and didn't care. His house was empty. He was alone, abandoned. He had told Gwen, neat and pinched in her travelling clothes, that for all he cared she could bloody well never come back. But he felt as though he had been mangled by lions. His heart was torn apart in great bleeding pieces. When Eleanor opened the door he swayed on the doorstep and almost fell into her arms.

Ellis's drunkenness always went through predictable phases, all linked by rage, until the final, somnulent plunge into self-pity. He began by being amusing, witty and clear-headed; a bout of rage then led him to the working class, their sterling qualities and the abomination of men working in eighteen-inch seams—at this point he was pure nineteenth century and wore a metaphorical cloth cap and muffler, burning against the injustices of the Industrial Revolution; two more whiskies and he was a Trotskyite in Eastern Europe, a devotee of Castro, a revolutionary in Peru—all his heroes were murdered, or being tortured in Fascist prisons, they died in a useless attempt to absolve his guilt, which was immeasurable. At this point he often wept, and women would try to comfort him, which led to a phase of incoherent amorousness in which he would propose marriage to anyone who happened to be sitting at his knee. Soon after this the tragic head would droop, the glass fall out of his hand; the women would tiptoe away, only to be summoned back by a stentorian shout of 'Don't leave me! Why are you all leaving me?' Eleanor was one of the few who did leave, kissing his tormented head and sometimes covering him with a blanket.

In the morning he would usually be gone, having muttered and blundered his way through the dawn in the general direction of his home, and the numbly waiting Gwen.

Tonight there was no waiting Gwen and his sense of loneliness was dangerous. She put the bottle of whisky beside him, but he remained sullen and withdrawn. He execrated the harmless Gwen, mumbling that all was over between them, if she wanted to go off to that bloody Stalinist country —history, as usual, had become confused—she could bloody well stay there. For the first time since she had known him she could find no contact, no means of shocking him into life. He was a sodden, immovable bore, his chin sunk on his chest, his great corduroy legs sprawled like a stranded doll. For the first time, also, she had the feeling that he cared nothing for her; that he didn't even see her. She was an unwelcome guest in her own sitting room and would have been less lonely alone.

She heard a key turning in the lock of the front door, the front door slamming. Jessica, perhaps? But there was no rushing and scampering of Juniper, let loose from the carpet bag. 'If she doesn't give a shit for me,' Ellis was growling, 'why doesn't she get the hell out? I'll tell you why she doesn't get the hell out. Because she lives on me. That's why. Because she's a crawling parasite.'

Eleanor made a perfectly accurate comment. 'You're broken-hearted,' she said.

'Broken-hearted. Yes. In small pieces, but who the hell's going to sweep me up. Eh?'

Cressida came in. Her long dark hair, so unlike Daphne's smooth sheets, was tangled and her eyes, enormous, bottle green, looked coldly at the drunk man in the chair. Like Eleanor, she seldom wore what could be called clothes: her jeans were baggy at the knees and her loose shirt had lost a button. She had come from Putney, where she had been visiting a friend with a six-month-old baby. She had played with the baby timidly, as though the robust creature might break at her touch. The friend's husband had come back just before she left. She had felt like a carol singer who, having piped her song, glimpses a warm world before the door is shut in her face. That Putney house was home. This was a cold house where her mother, looking bored and uncomfortable, was entertaining a drunkard.

'Come in,' Ellis said testily. 'Don't hang about. I know I'm drunk, but I'm not bloody diseased.'

Eleanor gave her a look of despair and apology. Soft-hearted to the point of weakness, Cressida came and sat down on the sofa. She had known Ellis since she was thirteen, and some of his paintings filled her with awe. She understood why Eleanor was fond of him, but she was afraid of drunkenness, of violence and noise. As though realising this, Ellis completely changed his manner. From the moment Cressida accepted his invitation—or, rather, obeyed his command—all his innate gentleness rose to the surface, he smiled, he was articulate, he was charming.

'You look all wind-blown and shining,' he said. 'Where have you been?'

She said she had been to Putney, which made him laugh quietly, as though a voyage to Putney were both humorous and endearing. Eleanor noticed that he had stopped drinking, the glass of whisky by his side remained untouched. The congested, enraged face regained its devastated handsomeness. He questioned Cressida, persuaded her out of her reticence, made her laugh with her head bent down to hide it, showing her small, uneven teeth. Eleanor watched and listened and accepted without rancour the fact that Cressida, by the fact of her careless and mysterious youth, had accomplished something which, she, the old and trusted friend, could never have managed. She saw Cressida's sombreness and disappointment being slowly transformed into delight. In the weeks to come, she thought, they would sometimes take Cressida with them, allow her to join their holiday. It would do her good. She smiled with them both, warmly approving.

Ellis suggested that they all went out to dinner. Eleanor said there was food in the house, but the way in which he ridiculed the idea of cooking and washing up reminded her of the days when he would dismiss her entire life as 'bourgeois'. The three of them walked, with Ellis keeping a steady straight line between them, to a nearby bistro which had been opened to cater for the prosperous young marrieds in regimented rows of neo-Georgian cottages, each with their garage and their *au pair* girl and their colour television set. It was nearly always empty, the young marrieds, for some unfathomable reason, preferring to stay at home. Eleanor had doubts about the freshness of the food, but kept them to herself.

Ellis sat next to Cressida; Eleanor, feeling more and more like a duenna, opposite them. Cressida seldom drank wine, and now her lips and cheeks were tinged with colour, her eyelids becoming heavier over the extraordinary cat eyes. Looking at her, Eleanor found herself wondering with strange detachment why she loved her so much. Like the vampire, she has been dead many times, and has learned the secrets of the grave. Supposing she told them that she had once learned the whole of Pater's description of the Mona Lisa by heart and revelled in it? Supposing she told them that she existed? Cressida had some quality of being able to move between life and death like a spectre; usually she chose the shades, the immobility, the apathy of barely breathing; now, leaning towards Ellis, emphasising a point with a stubby, capable hand, she was suddenly the most beautiful and alert of all Eleanor's children. Pride and sadness were confused. She wanted to go away, to be metamorphosed, to become invisible. Ellis ordered another bottle of wine.

'I think,' she said, 'I'll go home. I'm dreadfully sleepy.'

They noticed her, arranging their faces in slight dismay. 'Oh, don't go . . .'

'I'll come too,' Cressida said.

'No, you won't,' Ellis said. 'You'll stay and finish this

bottle of wine.' He put his hand over Eleanor's fondly. 'If your mum's tired, let her go to bed.'

'Are you sure?' Cressida asked.

'Of course. See you later.' She kissed Ellis's bristly cheek. 'Call me,' she said.

'Of course I'll call you.'

She walked home down the street of closed, brightly lit shops, the delicatessen and the launderette, the ironmonger's with bright green lawnmowers on raffia grass, the news-agent's and the watch-mender's. She crossed the roundabout, uncertainly waiting for cars that waited, uncertainly, for her. She started up the darker street that led to her house. The pubs were emptying and once more she saw the girl in the PVC raincoat, pausing for a moment in the glare of the saloon bar as though waiting for someone. At the corner of the street she took her keys out of her pocket and felt for the right one. She looked up at the house. It was dark, but Jessica would probably be in her room at the back. She climbed the steps slowly and let herself in. Immediately she sensed the absence, not so much of Jessica, but of Juniper. Cold, black, unin-habited, there was nothing to welcome or even resent her. She switched on the kitchen light. Patrick June 1st? Swept by a sudden wave of tenderness she went to Philip's room and turned down Cressida's bed, drew the curtains, laid out the nightdress and slippers, left the bedside light on in case, when the girl came home, she should feel uncared for.

10

Mrs. Bennet was fertilising her roses. She had fed them well with warm, hairy manure in January, shovelling it into her wheelbarrow from a nearby farmyard, but this May feeding was a kind of dessert which she felt they appreciated. Not partial to dogs or cats, she anthropomorphised her Fragrant Clouds and Lilli Marlenes and Anna Wheatcrofts. She did not exactly attribute personalities to them, although the Charles de Mills in the centre bed certainly looked as though it was going to be more aggressive than the Penelope in the west border. She did think that, probably more than most people, they had souls. If she had been asked what she meant by a soul she would have dismissed the question as though soul were as much an ingredient of life as salt or cinnamon or baking powder. The appearance of a soul was attenuated, limbless, and it soared perpetually upward. The smell of her roses when she buried her nose in them was soul. She regarded orthodox religion as ridiculous, except as a tonic for children, but was devoted to nature.

As she sprinkled the nutritious powder over the roots of her loved ones, and watered it well in, she thought, as she did continually, of her family. 'What are we going to do about Nelly?' was again, after nearly forty years, an absorbing question. If only the girl would take up some time-consuming work, visit the sick or read to the blind or knit bootees for Vietnamese babies. If only, Mrs. Bennet thought, straightening herself with difficulty and looking across her flowered and wooded acres, the girl could see *out*. She herself had always seen out; it did not occur to her that apart from staring into the damp scented hearts of her roses, she had never seen in. At eighty-two, although physically she seemed as tough as a jobbing gardener, she was beginning to soften, to crinkle and pucker round the edges. Until bitterness can be purged, she thought surprisingly, as though suddenly struck on the road to Damascus, there can be no well-being. She bent again to her task.

Cressida, now, had a weak chest and had always been inclined to constipation. She doubted whether anyone was dealing with these ailments, and certainly when the child had come down to stay a few weeks ago she looked peaky and had a very nasty cough. If only she would get a job and give up the idea of this unsuitable American. Where had she lost them, Cressida and Daphne? Why, like other girls of their age, weren't they engaged or married and pregnant? She wanted great-grandchildren, great-grand-daughters whom she could dose and spoil and walk with in her rose garden. Daphne's young man had been perfectly dreadful, with hair like a fuzzy-wuzzy and dark glasses, though it had been raining at the time of their visit. There must be nice young men in the world, young architects and lawyers and . . . well, suitable young men with prospects. Was it Graham's fault? She refused even to think about Graham, dismissing him with her most pejorative epithet: 'a typical man'. Most men, except Mr. Bennet, the late Lord Russell, Malcolm Muggeridge and Sir Kenneth Clark, were 'typical men': gross in their habits, obsessed by sex, deceitful, vain and, worst of all, little boys at heart. It was probably not surprising, after all, that her two eldest grand-daughters, aged twenty-two and twenty-four, remained spinsters.

Then, of course, there was Jessica. She did not criticise

Jessica, as Mrs. Strathearn did; in fact she felt very warmly towards her, and thought the tacked-up pre-Raphaelite dresses and huge patchwork shawls rather becoming. Somehow, although she didn't know how, there was a connection between Jessica and the roses; both emanated an intangible and perfumed spirit that she might, if she had been that sort of woman, have called hope. She had never been very close to Jessica, and did not know about the boys whom, with true generosity, Jessica wrapped in her arms. She believed in Jessica. With a rare stab of loneliness she wished Jessica were here now with that silly little puppy; or, as she had promised, with some of her charges whom Mrs. Bennet irresistibly thought of as 'slum children'.

As for Philip, the most one could hope would be that he would turn out to be a gentleman. Marcus—she slammed her mind firmly shut—was a closed book. She had begotten, and raised—and possibly ruined—a race of woman. She was perpetually concerned with them. She passionately wanted Eleanor's manless home to succeed and was only waiting for her Italian gardener, Franco, to come and mow the lawn before she set out for London to see for herself, and contribute what she thought necessary.

For some reason her work with the roses, and her busy thoughts about her family, had left her unusually tired. She went indoors, carefully changed her shoes and made herself a cup of Bovril. She must have slept for a while in her high wing chair, slippered feet on a footstool, hands seamed with garden earth open on her lap. She didn't hear the car, or the front door opening, or Eleanor coming into the room. When she woke, Eleanor was sitting in the opposite chair, watching her.

'Oh dear!' she exclaimed, momentarily frightened out of her wits. Then, 'My dear child, what on earth are you doing?'

Eleanor smiled. 'Nothing. I didn't want to wake you.'

'I wasn't asleep,' the old lady lied. 'You do creep about so.'

'I'm sorry. How are you?'

'Extremely well. I've just been feeding the roses. Is any thing wrong?'

'No,' Eleanor said. 'It was a nice day. I just felt like coming.'

One liar can recognise another. Mrs. Bennet said nothing but put all problems on one side like knitting, to be resumed later.

'I'll see what we've got for lunch,' she said. ' I wish you'd let me know you were coming.'

'I really don't want anything,' Eleanor said ineffectually

But they had cold lamb and new potatoes and cold apple pie. Eleanor, who for some time had needed a moderate amount of drink, had brought a bottle of wine. Mrs. Bennet found her daughter tense and uncommunicative and kept urging her to have another glass, as though it were Wincarnis or Sanatogen, which she knew, from her own experience, were good for the nerves. At last, when they had washed up, Mrs. Bennet put a match to the expertly laid fire, which blazed in a moment, and said, 'Well, now, child. What's the trouble?'

Instead of strengthening her, putting her in her right place as a grown woman, expecting her to be rational and in control, Mrs. Bennet was, with a kind of instinctive and unconscious cunning, reducing Eleanor to a helpless dependent. After Eleanor's initial resistance, when she went through the usual defences of 'Oh, nothing . . . it's not important . . . It's really nothing . . .' she at last said, 'Well. You know Ellis—Ellis Cromer.'

'The painter,' Mrs. Bennet snapped, as though on a quiz programme.

'Yes. But you met him once . . . I brought him to see you.'

'Yes. I remember. A very large man, I think he was in love with you or something.'

'Well. That was a long time ago.' There was a long pause. Eleanor dragged her hands down the lower part of her face, as though adjusting it. 'He's started having an affair with Cressida.'

'*Cressida?*'

'Yes.'

Mrs. Bennet asked the one question which was impossible to answer: 'But . . . *why?*'

'He . . . he lives with a girl. I like her, she's called Gwen. She's gone to Russia on some student trip or something. So,' she finished lamely, 'he's taken up with Cressida.'

For the next five minutes she hardly listened. It was enough to have the warm outrage washing over her, to hear all the Bennet wails of calamity which she could not utter herself—being too cowardly or too aware?—and to watch, curiously detached, the Bennet grandmother both execrating and excusing her young.

'But that,' she said finally, when the old lady had trembled to a halt, 'isn't the point.'

'Isn't the point?'

'You see . . . I suppose it was silly . . . But I had thought, hoped that Ellis and I might . . . Well, that we might be friends. Now suddenly it's terribly complicated.'

'Yes,' Mrs. Bennet said, without fully understanding. 'Of course it is.'

'And I don't want Cressida to think that I disapprove . . .'

'Of course you disapprove! The man's old enough to be her father, dissolute, a drunkard . . .' Eleanor had often thought how well Mrs. Bennet would have done in public life at the beginning of the century. Enormously hatted, ballooned into a shirt-waister, button-booted and brandishing a gamp, she would have made modern women's liberation movements look like a club for infant television viewers.

'No,' she said. 'Ellis is . . . a good man. He's just confused.'

'No man is a good man who can take up Cressida as though she were a . . .' Even Mrs. Bennet couldn't say 'woman of the streets', so she made do with 'well, I mean, a plaything . . .'

'I don't think he's done that. They were both lonely.'

'But so were you,' Mrs. Bennet said, hitting the nail exactly on the head.

'Yes . . . But it's not the same.' It was, of course, precisely the same. It was the hideous situation of finding herself in competition with Cressida—could it really be as crude as that?—that so immensely distressed her. And, worse, the fact that she could never be in competition with Cressida, but must give way gracefully, with love, pretending that nothing was being taken from her. Ellis's contemporary, Cressida's mother, she felt that she must give them her blessing and let them go. As always, anger, unrighteous and irrational indignation, was not available to her.

'Well, anyway,' she said, 'it's a mess. I wanted to get away from it for a bit.'

'Will you stay the night?'

'No.' That was going too far. Jessica, who had been away for three days, might come home. Cressida might come home, to find the bed still turned down, the nightdress ready, but the bedside light turned off. She didn't want them to meet a dark and empty house.

'Shall I come back with you?' Mrs. Bennet asked. Only she knew what a sacrifice this was, with the lawn unmown and Franco without instructions, half of her roses left without their food.

Eleanor had come here in order to feel like a child. Mrs. Bennet had succeeded admirably, the humiliation of Graham's, Kilcannon's, Alex's and now Ellis's desertion was eased, she almost felt too young to concern herself with men. Mrs. Bennet would be a buffer between Cressida and herself; she might even, as she would put it, take Ellis to task. There would be breakfast and lunch and even tea. There would be knitting in the evenings, and advice about her derelict garden. Above all, her confusion, the widening wound of her loneliness, would be staunched.

'Yes, please,' she said, leaving it at that.

The old lady was adept at packing. She had been to the rescue so often attending five births and innumerable attacks of measles, whooping cough, chicken-pox and Eleanor's rare but always surprising attacks of exhaustion. She packed one cardigan, one best woollen dress, two pairs of silk directoire knickers, one vest, two pairs of lisle stockings, nightdress, dressing gown, slippers, sponge bag, hairbrush and a packet of Marie biscuits in case she felt hungry in the night. It was all done in ten minutes. She left Franco a note printed in capital letters about mowing the lawn and fertilising the roses; she left another, more intimate, note for her charwoman about feeding the cat and cleaning the upstairs windows. She then put on her coat and round, rather rakish, felt hat and said she was ready to go.

And Eleanor, as she started up the car with her small mother tucked in beside her, felt defeated.

II

The legal side of the tragi-comedy crept forwards—and
backwards—as though a simple Deed of Separation were
Penelope's tapestry; all that Messrs. Rothman, Bich and Bite
did by day was unravelled by Messrs. Crookston, Push and
Mandeville by night. Enormous demands were made by Bich
and Bite, at Rothman's instigation, which were indignantly,
though courteously, refused by Mandeville and Push. Decor-
ous raspberries were blown by Crookston at Bich. In the
middle of it all Graham's accountant, a harrassed man with a
poetical soul, sorted through tax demands and spectacular
expenses and unpaid fees as though his life depended on it;
which, in part, it did. Graham's new secretary, an ex-model
whose fingernails got trapped in the typewriter keys, was told
to say 'No' to everything, regardless. Graham himself took
very little part in the proceedings, though the idea of giving
away money for nothing filled him with a burning, indigest-
ible rage. When Push rang up one day and asked whether Dr.
Strathearn would be averse to paying his wife £3500 a year
tax-free, Trixy, the secretary, obediently said 'No'. When
Graham was presented with a draft deed in which this sum
was mentioned he screamed—the pitch was far too high to
be called a shout—and tore the offending document into small
pieces. Then all he could think of was to telephone his ac-

countant, who was trying to trap a couple of lines of Tennyson in the back of his figure-encumbered brain. Somewhere deep inside himself the accountant felt near tears. He telephoned Bite and he telephoned Push. The whole business started again from the beginning.

In the meanwhile Eleanor was running out of money. Except in her very rare eruptions of rage, she sincerely did not want money from Graham. It was not a matter of principle—she had no particular belief in independence and reckoned, if she thought about it, that she had earned her keep for the past twenty-six years. It was a matter of love, and the almost sibling relationship between money and love. No love—no money. It was as simple as that. If she resented Graham spending money on Nell Partwhistle, it was the love she was resenting, not the Diners Cards and Barclaycards and American Express cards and small pink cheques that were the tokens of wealth. Like an ignorant child she wished—and almost believed—that she could live on air.

She was, therefore, the despair of Messrs. Rothman, Bich and Bite. She didn't answer their letters or their telephone calls. She only once went to see them, when she was interviewed by Bite, who kept a large golden labrador under his desk and had the air of a man about to become a mystic. He told her, in a far-away voice, that she was entitled to the house, the custody of Philip, and approximately—his voice became an echo from a distant mountainside—£5000 a year. She could also divorce Graham for adultery, cruelty and, in due course, desertion. She said she didn't want to divorce Graham. He and the labrador both sighed. She went away, never to return.

Inconsistently, perhaps, she was almost obsessive about paying bills immediately they arrived; possibly because she had always paid them with someone else's money. Now she found that she was spearing the bills on a hook in the kitchen, where they fluttered in the draught and became stained with steam and spitting fat. The tradesmen, many of whom had known her for a number of years, since they had all lived in the house half a mile away, began to look a little pained. If I can live without money, her dream self thought, so can they. Her conscious self was worried and despicably—she felt—helpless. She began to notice that Jessica could eat three pounds of apples a day, and that Juniper got through four pounds of stewing steak a week. The record player, the suitable tray and the wine—now considerably diminished—were an accusation. She was able to economise because Mrs. Bennet, when Eleanor was a child, had taught her to economise. But she could not stand in a queue for apples at 9p when she could buy them speedily in the supermarket at 10p. She could not stop smoking, or drinking her white Mâcon at 69p a bottle. She bought no clothes because in this curiously cloistered life she didn't need them. If Graham had given her a cheque for £100 inside a greetings card, or a cheque for £1000 with a warm kiss, she would have accepted them readily. As it was, she had not the will, or the anger, or the conviction, to get blood out of a stone.

Graham, as it happened, was not mean. He simply objected to having money extorted from him by law. He also had an unreasonable fantasy that Eleanor, who had spent three months at an art school in her teens, should go out to work. Only Nell Partwhistle, sitting about all day brushing her hair, was exempt from work. His women patients—that is, the women who could afford to have him for a doctor—were either profitably married (though always unhappily), or profitably divorced, or, most profitably of all, they worked: that is, they were film stars, actresses, television executives, best-selling novelists, screen writers or, more simply and honestly, tarts. He could not understand why a woman with whom he no longer lived, let alone slept with, should be financially dependent on him. He agreed to Bite's faint demand that he should give Jessica £10 a week. When Jessica heard of this she continued to eat apples and to feed the carnivorous Juniper, but a dream drifted into her head and she went, dreaming, to find Brian

on somebody's broken-down sofa or lying snug and at ease
on somebody's bathroom floor.

Little by little, a supreme detector of any kind of discomfort, Mrs. Bennet began to understand this situation. Assisted
by Daphne, whose practical mind lay like ice over troubled
water, she sorted out the financial situation, found it outrageous, and threatened to tackle Graham.

'Please, Mother,' Eleanor pleaded. 'It wouldn't do any
good. It's under control.'

'His control,' Daphne snapped. 'You need a real beast of
a lawyer, not this useless Bite.'

'If I need money,' Eleanor said softly, 'I know he'll give
it to me.'

'You do need it, and he's not.' And do stop being such a
bloody drip, Daphne thought.

'Well, anyway . . .' More and more frequently, this phrase
was becoming her comment on life. Alex had, in a way, left
her for Georgina: well, anyway . . . Cressida spent most of
her days and nights with Ellis: well, anyway . . . Graham,
according to Mrs. Bennet and Daphne, was behaving in an
inhuman, if not brutal, fashion: well, anyway . . . Philip
had not written since he went back to school: well, anyway
. . . The writing on the wall said that Kilcannon was coming
on June 1st: well, anyway . . . With Mrs. Bennet in residence,
sleeping in Jessica's theatrical room, the crust of Eleanor's
identity seemed to crumble. She wandered, she was vague, she
forgot things, the simple tasks of buttering bread or straightening cushions seemed too much for her. She had collapsed
against Mrs. Bennet's strength; she had become, as she had
always become with her mother, emasculated. Some small,
harsh voice in her insisted that she should send Mrs. Bennet
away. She heard it, but did not listen. She was resigned, everyone except her mother having left her, to acting the part of a
retarded child.

.   .   .   .   .

'She must go,' Cressida said. 'She *must* go.'

'But Nell would be so alone,' Ellis said, slightly maudlin.

'Then she must bloody well be alone, mustn't she?' The voice low and hesitant, was Cressida's; the sentiment, Daphne's.

'Oh, come here and stop bothering yourself, you're like a fucking gramophone record.'

'You know what she did?' Cressida asked, muffled in his blue denim. 'She paid all the bills.'

'Who did?'

'Grandmother Bennet. Without telling Mother. It's horrible.'

'Couldn't we talk about me for a change. I'm still here, you know.'

She kissed him, thinking of Tom McGraw.

'Shall we have a baby?' he asked, pronouncing it 'babby'.

'Do you want one?' she asked, thinking of Tom McGraw.

'I've always wanted one. There's a child in every painting I do. Have you noticed that? You haven't noticed that, have you?'

'No,' she said.

'No. You wouldn't. What's painting to you? A postcard you buy in the bloody National Gallery to send to your mother. If you're away from your mother, that is. Which is infrequent.'

She stretched herself from him, walking, hugging herself, round the overheated studio. 'I hate you when you talk like that.'

'All right, then. Bloody well hate me. See if I care.' He poured himself another drink. Since Gwen's departure he had seldom been sober.

'What about your mother, then?'

'Dead. And me father's a bloody carbuncle,' he chortled. 'A bloody carbuncle on God's foot.'

'Very clever,' she said, 'and it means absolutely nothing, nothing at all.'

'Oh, for God's sake . . .' He was suddenly dreadfully tired. 'Shall I paint you?'

'If you like.'

'If *I* like? I asked you what *you'd* like. Don't you exist, or something?'

'Yes. And I'm going.'

'Back to Mother?'

'She's your . . . friend!' Cressida blazed. '*You* loved her! *You* wanted to take her away and marry her and have a baby and God knows what! How dare you talk about her like that?'

'It's true. It's true.' His head fell sideways, his mouth crumpled. 'I loved her all right. God, I did love her. It was only that bloody doctor that got in the way. Your dad. He's a trivial man, your dad. No offence meant, and all that. You know what he once said to me? "Cromer," he said, "I would willingly let you marry my wife, but you are not a good risk." What d'you think he meant by that?'

'I don't know.'

'Not a good risk. What risk is a good risk, anyway? Where are you going?'

She had slung her handbag over her shoulder, put on her dark glasses.

'I'm going home.'

'Oh, come on . . .' He put out a restraining hand, but couldn't reach far enough. 'What shall I do, left here all on me tod? Probably drink myself to death, that's what I'll do.' The genuine, gentle voice came through: 'Don't leave me, Cressie.'

'I must.' She did love him, in a way, though he exhausted her to the point of tears. He was so different from Tom McGraw that they might not have been the same species. She was not strong-willed, and it was very difficult to leave him. She had left Tom McGraw, and would not lose sight of the purpose. Loving with Tom had been a sterile ecstasy. With Ellis it was a rough and tumble in which at any moment they might find themselves playing in a jungle of babies. She held his head between her hands and kissed his forehead. 'Ring me. Or come round when you're sober.'

'She doesn't want to see me.' He was nearly in tears.

'Of course she wants to see you. She needs to see you. She needs to see people.'

'And what about that old termagent—Grandma?'

'I'm going to send her away.'

'The hell you are. She'll stick like a bloody limpet. You monstrous regiment of women . . .'

'Ring me,' she said again, and before she went out of the door she said, 'Do some work.'

'Work! You desert me, abandon me, leave me to Christ knows what horrors, and you tell me to work . . .'

She closed the door on the wretched voice and groped her way down the stairs. Outside it was a beautiful May afternoon. She hurried along under the trees, responsible, vital, determined to get rid of her grandmother and save her mother's life.

.   .   .   .   .

Jessica let herself in through the front door very quietly, carrying Juniper so that the puppy would not scamper and scuffle across the hall. She listened, but there was no sound except the ticking of the kitchen clock. She tiptoed upstairs to the sitting room, still carrying Juniper, and looked round the door. Eleanor was lying on the sofa with her eyes closed. Jessica put Juniper down and asked diffidently, 'Are you asleep?'

Eleanor opened her eyes and smiled, her hand wrestling with the excited puppy. 'No.' She sat up, pushing back her hair. 'What's the time?'

'I don't know. About four. Where's Grandmother Bennet?'

'She went shopping. Then I think she was going to see some friend in . . . I don't know, Earls Court.'

'Good.' Jessica sat down on the edge of an armchair, nursing Juniper on her lap. 'Because I want to talk to you.'

Eleanor reached for a cigarette. She felt pleased and apprehensive.

'Then talk.'

'Well . . .' The effort of expressing herself in speech, rather than in touch or dance or paint or love, flushed her cheeks. 'Well . . . you know Brian?'

'Yes.' He had been to the house two or three times, silent but not uncivil.

'Well . . .' it came out in a rush, 'he wants me to go and live with him.'

The pause was too long. What ought I to say was in conflict with what do I want to say. Finally she asked, 'Where?'

'He's got a room in St. Stephen's Gardens. It's only two pounds a week. And it's near the playground.'

Irrelevantly Eleanor said, 'You won't be working in the playground for ever.'

'No. I want to work with mentally handicapped children. The training centre is near there too.'

Eleanor looked at her and loved her as another person might have loved a poem, a painting, a theme of music. She loved her with awe, and with the sense that she must not in any way, by the slightest indication of misunderstanding, spoil the thing she loved.

'Do you love Brian?' she asked.

'Oh, yes.'

'And he . . . ?'

'Yes.'

'And what about money?'

'He has a grant . . .' Jessica said, vague for the first time.

'And . . . that's what you both want to do?'

'Very much.'

'Well, then,' Eleanor said, with a smile that looked tender but felt like a rictus, 'that's what you must do.'

But Jessica, struggling, needed to explain herself further.

'I know you've got this house and all . . . I mean, for us. I feel a bit beastly, really. And of course I'll come and see you, I'll often come and see you . . . But, you see, I think I'm a bit too old or something . . . Well, not really old, but it's like our ways of life . . . well, they aren't really the same, are they? I mean, I think this is a lovely house. For you. But I'll feel happier in a room, honestly I will. And'—she rushed into a spurt of laughter, in case Eleanor should be feeling sad— 'you won't have Juniper peeing all over the place . . .'

Through her children, more than through any lover or husband, Eleanor had learned to weep behind a smiling face. Even her eyes remained dry. She said quite calmly, 'I shall miss Juniper. When do you plan to go?'

'Well . . . tomorrow, if that's all right. Brian's got a friend who's got a truck so I can take all my stuff and everything . . .'

So it was all arranged. One more question: 'Have you told . . . Graham?'

'No. But he won't care much anyway, will he?'

'I think you should tell him.'

'All right. If you think so. We're going down to the country with them on Sunday anyway. Nell's father's got what she calls a country estate. You'll like it, won't you, Juniper?' She ruffled the dog's head, asking it a direct—and, to Eleanor, bitterly cruel—question.

'Let's have tea,' Eleanor said. 'Grandmother B. made an enormous chocolate cake.'

.   .   .   .   .

The confrontation between Cressida and Mrs. Bennet came late in the evening. Jessica was doing what she called packing, throwing her possessions into the same tea chests that she had used when she moved in to what was to have been her new home. Eleanor, innocently falling in with a plan made by Cressida, had gone out to dinner with Ellis, who had severely sobered himself up for the occasion. Cressida and

Mrs. Bennet watched television until the old lady, with a snort of disgust, asked Cressida to turn it off.

'Such rubbish!' she said, heaving up her knitting. 'They must think we're all morons.'

It was delicate ground, because Cressida had not really had it out with her grandmother about Ellis. The problems, therefore, might get confused.

'When are you thinking of going home?' she asked casually.

'I don't know, dear. When your mother no longer needs me.'

'Of course she needs you,' Cressida said diplomatically. 'We all need you. But don't you think it might be better . . . if we had somewhere to go to? I mean, when you're here we're sort of . . . stuck.'

Mrs. Bennet paused in her knitting. She was by no means stupid.

'What do you mean, darling—"stuck"?'

'Well, your house, and you in your house, means an awful lot to us. Look at the way Mother went down to see you the other day . . .'

'A fortnight ago,' the old lady corrected.

'Yes. And I came down for the night. And Daphne goes to see you. When you're here we're sort of . . . cut off. We've got nowhere to go to.'

'It seems very peculiar reasoning,' Mrs. Bennet said, puzzled.

'No. It's not. I know there are times when Mother would like to . . . well, escape. If you're here, where can she escape to? Do you see what I mean? Of course, it's lovely having you here, but you'd be much more use'—she used the word advisedly, knowing it was the one which would most sharply penetrate her grandmother's conscience—'if you were down in the country, where we could come and stay. Particularly now it's summer.'

Mrs. Bennet was capable of a certain contained merriment.

'I think you're trying to get rid of me,' she said, and twinkled.

'Of course not. But Mother's got to get used to living alone . . .'

'I don't like it,' the old lady interrupted firmly.

'Well, anyway, I'm here, and Philip will soon be home for the holidays.'

'You seem to spend most of your time,' Mrs. Bennet said, *touché*, 'with Ellis Cromer.'

'That's got nothing to do with it. Anyway, it won't last. Gwen will be home soon and then . . .'

'And then what?'

'I don't know. But it's got nothing to do with Mother.' That, she knew, was a lie. 'The point is . . . that she's got to find out how she's going to live. And while you're here she just . . . drifts.'

Mrs. Bennet used her intelligence. She did not understand very much of what her grand-daughter said. But there were the roses, the problems of greenfly, black spot, mildew and rust. It was nearly June, and the garden cried out to her. How much more pleasant to have Eleanor staying with her than to try to keep a firm hand on this tall house, with its endless stairs and her grand-daughters' incomprehensible and vaguely unpleasant sex problems.

'Perhaps you're right, dear,' she said. 'I was going to do some baking tomorrow. Jessica seems very fond of treacle tart, and you can always do with some rock cakes. I'll go on Saturday.'

Cressida could not bring herself to explain that if Jessica was going to eat the treacle tart she would share it with Brian on the floor of some room in Notting Hill Gate. She had done enough. Suddenly she missed Ellis, and felt a shock of something like jealousy that he was having dinner with Eleanor while she, his momentary mistress, was alone. She went down to her room and started a letter to Tom: 'Dear Tom, I miss you very much tonight and the world of home seems altogether too difficult and complicated for me . . .'

12

Cressida had been right. From the moment Mrs. Bennet left, some part of Eleanor revived. Even the loss of Jessica and Juniper did not seem unduly to disturb her. Cressida, sensing that there might be some sort of eruption, which equally might be avoided, kept constant watch. Her problems with Ellis were kept for the night-time, when Eleanor was asleep. The three of them spent many evenings together, curiously domestic, with Ellis carving the joint and Cressida making the coffee, almost a family, although the roles they were playing were rather confused. Daphne, coming in on these peaceful, slightly boozy evenings, was a little shocked. The flaxen-haired Zulu had gone, to be replaced by Hereward, a pretty boy who did something rather vague in the world of pop music. For the first time in her life Daphne was desperately in love. She doted on him and told him how lovely he looked and washed his skinny shirts and his pastel bikini underpants; she cooked him exquisite meals, which she sat watching him eat, as though he were an Eastern potentate. Finally, being a determined girl who was paradoxically eaten by some parasite of fear, she gave the violinist notice and Hereward moved in. He did not realise it for a few weeks, but Daphne was going to marry him. She began to be very curt with the writer, leaving him on the dot of half past five in the middle of some crisis which he could not possibly solve. He complained about her bitterly, believing that this show of independence was some form of mental derangement.

It was the end of May. It was then, Eleanor realised with remote surprise, June 1st. Cressida was going to the theatre with Ellis, so she bought two steaks and some cheese and left it at that. Some vague memory of her infatuation with Kilcannon made her wash her hair and throw away a long-dead azalea. It was better like this, Cressida said. Things you look forward to are never successful. 'Just open the door and say hullo Knight and give him a zonking great whisky. He may even turn out to be quite nice.'

In the middle of the afternoon, when the telegram arrived, it was almost as though she had been expecting it: 'So sorry hospitalised may I ring you soon Patrick.' She rang Jessica and Brian, who for some unknown reason had a bright red telephone which they were continually losing under piles of books and Jessica's squirrel-hoards of material. She asked them to dinner, and Brian ate both steaks, while Jessica and Juniper ate the cheese. She was not sad. She was not even disappointed. It was as though some invisible, intangible, unknown being were teaching her a lesson. Write down a hundred times: this is what life is like, this is what life is going to be like. Repeat after me: expect nothing, do nothing, say nothing, simply be.

But she was not an apt pupil; she did not concentrate. Now Mrs. Bennet had gone, she was beginning to be alive again, and the liveliness had to take some shape, have some objective. The home had stopped growing. Things that had been put on the landings in April, with the idea of moving them somewhere else, were still there in June. There were still half a dozen unshaded light bulbs. There were cases in the basement still unpacked and pictures still waiting to be nailed to the walls. She didn't care. There was a stoppage. She had given up ringing the Answering Service with its now rather patient 'Nothing for you, Mrs. Strathearn'; or, almost worse, some complicated message from the window cleaner or a faint bleat from Rothman, Bich or Bite. She needed, actually wanted, to go out into the world. How to set about it? She rang an acquaintance, the wife of a doctor friend of Graham's. She didn't actually ask what she should do, but the point was taken.

'Go out and buy twenty dinner plates, darling, and always keep some champagne on ice. We'll have lunch one day. I'll ring you.'

Well, what did one do? Join something? Advertise in the *New Statesman*? Have a dinner party to which one would have to invite almost perfect strangers? She solved the problem in the same way that taking arsenic eventually solves pain. She telephoned Graham.

'Hullo,' he said, surprised, swivelling his chair round so that he was not actually confronting his, at the time, uncontrollably sobbing patient. 'How are *you*?'

'Fine. I'm thinking of going down to see Philip.'

'Oh, yes?' He dug in a drawer and produced a box of tissues which he pushed across his desk. 'Where will you stay? The Brompton Arms?'

'I suppose so. You . . . wouldn't like to come down?'

'For the weekend, you mean?'

'No. Well, if you liked. I thought lunch or something on Sunday.'

'Yes. Yes, I think that might be quite possible. I'll ring you back. All right?'

'All right.'

Oh, Graham; oh, Graham; damn you, Graham. The boiling sorrow came through her eyes, her hands, her trembling knees. She had effectively taken poison and this was the result. She rang Cressida at the studio. Ellis, sounding glum, answered.

'Hullo. I suppose you want to talk to your daughter.'

'Yes.' And she added, wretchedly, 'Please.'

There was a long pause. Ellis was saying, 'It's Nell. She wants to talk to her fuckin' daughter.'

'Why didn't you talk to her, then?'

109

'Because I'm not in the mood.'

Cressida wrapped herself in a blanket and went to the phone. Her voice was bright and wary. 'Hullo? Mum?'

There was another long pause. Cressida said, 'Hullo? Are you there? What's wrong?'

Eleanor said simply, 'Will you come home? Just for a bit.'

'Of course. I'll be there in ten minutes. Hang on.'

'Oh Gawd,' Ellis said, 'has she cut her little finger again or something?'

'How often have *you* rung me,' Cressida demanded, quickly dressing, 'saying you must see me now, this minute, this very second?'

'It's different.'

'Yes, because there's never anything wrong with you, and when I get here there are dozens of people, all rushed round to save your life. Well, she's got no one.'

'Why the hell's she got no one, for Christ's sake? She's a woman, isn't she? She's sexy, if you like the more mature type of female. She's got a few brains. What's the matter with the bloody woman? Why doesn't she find herself a good fuck and be done with it . . .'

And yet tonight, quite probably, he would come round and even sit with his arm round Eleanor, while she, Cressida, sat on the floor like a child and they talked of things long past, things she couldn't remember. Ellis's almost continual violence—she knew now that he loved Gwen as strongly as he was capable of loving anyone—and Eleanor's deepening confusion seemed to be like walls, growing relentlessly higher until sometimes she could hardly see the sky. She wanted to be alone, to amble, to run, to pick flowers and let them drop from her fingers, to lie down and have a baby as painlessly as Adam lost his rib. She was twenty-four and felt old, because she was incurably afflicted with concern.

When she got home Eleanor, for some reason that Cressida could perfectly understand, was cleaning out the fridge. Her lushed face and swollen eyes needed no questions.

'It's Dad, I suppose,' Cressida said, and put the kettle on.

Eleanor nodded, beating the ice out of the metal containers.

'What happened?'

'Nothing, really. I rang him to say that I might go down and see Philip.'

'A good idea,' Cressida said. 'To see Philip, I mean.'

'He thought . . . I was asking him for the weekend. Graham, I mean.'

'And were you?'

'I hadn't thought of it. So I asked him to come down to lunch.'

'But you think he might have come for the weekend—if you had asked him?'

'I don't know. I suppose so. I don't know. He just said all right, he'd ring me back.'

'Tea or coffee?'

'I don't know. Tea.'

'So what are you going to do?'

'I'll go down. I suppose he'll come if he wants to.'

'But only for lunch.'

'Yes, I expect only for lunch.'

'You know,' Cressida said, 'if that bloody Knight had turned up the other day and done his stuff, you wouldn't have rung Dad, you wouldn't have given him a thought. Don't you see? It's not Dad. It's just *someone*.'

'Let's not talk about it,' Eleanor said. 'Do you want some chocolate cake?'

'No. But *let's* talk about it.' Cressida sat down firmly like an inquisitor. Eleanor fidgeted about the kitchen. 'What do you want from Dad? Love. Well, in a way you've got that because in a way he's potty about you and always will be. Everyone knows that. But he's not going to give you a damn thing and all his problems in life, which are practically invisible anyway, are solved by Nell Partwhistle. So where does that leave you?'

'Here,' Eleanor said.

'Exactly. And he's there, and that's how it's got to be. What d'you think you'd gain if he came down for the weekend, anyway?'

Eleanor didn't answer.

'You'd be miserable and wretched and buggered up and you'd have to separate all over again and you'd be back at square one.'

'Where did you learn all this?' Eleanor asked wryly, blowing her nose.

'At Grandmother Bennet's knee. No. I didn't learn it. It's just obvious. If you talked to me like this about Tom I should be just as . . . stupid.'

'Yes,' Eleanor said. 'You probably would. But you're right. And thank you.'

'Don't be idiotic. Do you want Ellis to take us out to supper?'

'No.'

'I don't either. Let's watch something perfectly ghastly on television. Something quite unspeakable. Like David Frost.'

·   ·   ·   ꝉ   §

The Brampton Arms was a four-star hotel built on the shore of a small lake which, whatever the season, was ruffled by a north wind. Its clientele was divided between company directors who came with their secretaries for the weekend and attended the Saturday-night dinner-dance, and the parents and relatives of children at Philip's school who, though often immensely distinguished, embarrassed the management by their clothes and their derisory comments about the Muzak in the toilets. It was also disturbing that the husbands seldom came with the wives, or the wives with the husbands. Each child appeared to have four parents, who vied with each other in providing lobster cocktails, fresh strawberries in January and even, on occasions, champagne. The manager had felt relatively safe with Dr. and Mrs. Strathearn. They were so very obviously married. Yet now Mrs. Strathearn came by herself, her pale face buried in a huge fur collar against the inclement June weather.

'Will Dr. Strathearn be joining you?' he asked, with a kind of undertone of sympathy.

'He'll be coming down for lunch tomorrow.'

'Ah. Such a busy doctor, I expect it's hard for him to get away.'

'Yes,' she said, and added, ridiculously, 'Summer 'flu.'

She drove the three miles to fetch Philip. Entering the school gates, she always felt in a different country, almost a different planet. Everyone was young. Even Philip's house-master was young enough to be her son. The buildings sprawled, apparently with no particular plan, over flat acres: spruce laboratories, sound-proof music rooms, workshops and studios. The old, mid-nineteenth-century part of the school had been built with an ecclesiastical as much as an academic vision: the Gothic arches, the cloisters, the silent cathedral of a library where the most rowdy children walked on tiptoe and could, if they felt inclined, read the works of John Updike and Philip Roth. She realised that she saw it quite differently from Philip, who scoffed and groaned and said he was only too glad to get away from the place. To Eleanor, educated in a minor public school where the only thing she had learned —because she was so frightened of it—was how to play hockey, this seemed a microcosm of reason and good sense in a chaotic world. She watched a girl, perhaps sixteen or seventeen, walking along the path with an armful of books: she wore a long dark skirt and boots, and her hair was like a sail; she walked straight, on the balls of her feet, as women must have walked centuries ago. A fair solid boy on a bicycle caught up with her, dismounted, and walked beside her. Eleanor wondered, in a futile, motherly way, how different her other children would have been if they had come to such a school. A tall, incredibly thin boy with hair down his back and his hands in his pockets sauntered towards the car. It took her nearly half a minute to recognise Philip. She opened the passenger door and as he bent to kiss her, hands still in his pockets, she saw that he had a soft smear of moustache on his upper lip; his eyes, behind the hairy curtain, were practically invisible.

'Hullo,' he said, settling himself. 'And how are you?'

'I'm very well. And how are you?'

'All right. Bloody glad to be out of that place.'

It was almost impossible, in these first moments after a long parting, to know what to talk about. Philip was remarkably helpful, asking questions about everyone except Graham, asking about the house, about the grandmothers. In two months he seemed to have grown two years. He told her there had been some fuss about smoking pot. She might hear about it, but she wasn't to believe a word she was told. Some ingenious fellow had rolled cigarettes out of a mixture of Balkan Sobranie, hay and nutmeg and had sold them for 12½p each. 'Remarkably effective they were, too,' Philip said. He put her at her ease, and by the time they arrived at the Brampton Arms she felt like a woman being taken out. He even held the swing doors open for her.

The waitresses, mini-skirted girls from New Zealand and Australia, were very partial to these schoolboys. They loved feeding them up, urging them on to more and more chips and whipped cream and frothing cider. Philip studied the menu extremely seriously. He was agonisingly torn between country-style pâté and avocado pear; desperately undecided between steak and grilled sole. At last, with the help of the bobbish waitress, he made up his mind. He ordered beer, so apparently the cider days were over. Eleanor, who had recently given up eating, played with a prawn cocktail and drank half a bottle of hock.

'Dad's coming down for lunch tomorrow.'

'Oh. Good.' Pause. 'Is he coming alone?'

She made a noise like laughing. 'I imagine so.'

114

'Good.' The country-style pâté took most of his attention. 'What's all this about Portugal?'

'Portugal?'

'He wrote and said he'd taken some house in Portugal or something for the summer.'

She knew her heart had momentarily stopped beating. 'It's the first I've heard of it.'

'Well, he wants me to go and stay. I suppose it'd be all right. But not for the whole time.'

'I don't know anything about it,' she said.

'I'd like to go to Greece for a couple of weeks. I could go on my own.'

'Would you mind'—it was a genuine, a serious question—'if I came with you?'

He finished off the pâté and swigged some beer. 'I should like that very much.'

'Good. Then we'll go to Greece.'

'We'll go north.' He spoke with the authority of an experienced traveller. 'After all, we've more or less done the south.' One miraculous Easter they had driven very slowly, stopping at every broken statue, from Olympia to Delphi. This, it seemed, was doing the south. 'I'd like to go to Meteora.'

'Meteora?'

'Those gigantic rocks with monasteries on the top. I like the sound of Meteora.'

'All right,' she said. 'That's what we'll do. Perhaps I should write to Marcus.'

'Why?' he asked, belligerent.

'Well . . . he knows all about Greece. He's stayed there a hundred times. He might give us . . . some advice.'

'Advice from Marcus,' he said, 'is something I can do without.'

She was charmed by the change in him. When the bill came he insisted on studying it carefully before she paid it. She could almost see him in ten—no, five—years' time, treating waiters with a sort of intimate insolence. She didn't approve of this, but as a woman she was delighted. They went into the lounge for coffee, where he picked up *Country Life* and was immediately immersed.

'You know you can buy an estate in Yorkshire with three cottages and a house with twelve bedrooms for £50,000?'

'Really?' she said. 'Do you want it?'

'Not particularly.' He leafed on, through Sheraton chairs and Chippendale davenports and Spode teapots.

'Do you want to go to the pictures?' she asked.

'Not particularly. Let's go for a walk.'

The usual light rain was falling. Eleanor thought of her soft bed, its silk eiderdown, with longing. If Graham had been here the two of them would have gone for a walk and she would have had a warm, womb-like, luxurious sleep before the ceremony of tea. She put on her coat and visored its collar.

'But you haven't got a raincoat ...'

'It doesn't matter.' He was wearing a black vest and denim jacket. He would get soaked. But it was no use fussing, so they set off round the pitted lake, with its swans sheltering in the reeds, the summer mud rising over his suède boots, the rain almost soothing in its steadiness.

'You know,' he said, 'I think it's all a very good thing.'

'What is?'

'I don't know,' he said, heaving a stone into the lake. 'Everything.'

She said very carefully, 'You seem much happier.'

'Yes. I am.'

Then they might as well talk. 'And what about Partwhistle?' She could never bear to say the girl's Christian name.

'What about her?' He skimmed a flat stone, bouncing it three times. 'She's all right.'

You don't feel *anything*? she wanted to ask. No loyalty? No anger for me? But before she could ask anything less

116

truthful, he had remarked, swinging on ahead of her a little, 'I don't see why you can't be more philosophical about all that.'

'Philosophical . . .' She repeated the word as though she were being trained to speak. 'You mean . . . why I can't put up with it . . . more easily?'

'Yes.' He was continually exercising himself, beating at the reeds or stretching for branches or throwing stones or simply turning, with his arms wide, almost as though dancing. 'I mean she's not important. She's just a girl.'

'Yes.'

'And she keeps Dad happy. Anyway, she keeps him quiet.'

'Yes.'

'I can't see what she's got to do with you. Really.'

'You can't.'

He bounded ahead, climbed on to a willow tree where he waited, his back against the trunk, as though leaning against a wall. The talk was over. They finished their walk round the lake and then had a huge tea of buttered toast and multi-coloured cakes. He said he had to go back to school to do some work, which was true and which she also believed. They drove back in a truly companionable silence, neither of them wondering what to say to the other.

'I'll come and fetch you tomorrow about eleven.'

'Why not let Dad come?'

She knew, without rancour, that he wanted to show off the Porsche.

'All right. I'll ring him and tell him to come earlier.'

He kissed her, circling her neck with his damp arm.

'Goodnight, then.'

'Goodnight, darling.'

She backed the car, and turned, before he had walked ten yards. Once, when she was a child, some interfering nursery governess had shown her a book which was meant to inform her about the female anatomy. It had been a fascinating book, with large coloured drawings with flaps that opened out showing the heart, lungs, intestines hidden beneath. One flap had opened on to a curled baby—surely, now she thought of it, three months old. She remembered this book for the first time in years as she drove through the country June evening. It was as though she were one of those drawings, and flaps were being opened by prying fingers, some of them her own. Many still remained closed, but the one that revealed itself now was called Parting. Some original, buried parting which she would never remember—the banishment, perhaps, from Mrs. Bennet's womb?—followed by an endless series of partings, her dying father (why did she so seldom think of him?), her school-friends, her few childhood sweethearts; then, one by one, her children, her lovers, Graham—and what was to come? Thirty more years of life at least; a parting lurking in each one of them? Was there to be no approaching, coming together; never a union? She did not specifically ask herself these questions; there was a questioning in her mind that was flavoured by them, the taste of a continual goodbye. She would see Philip tomorrow, but this evening's parting was indelible. She would part from him again tomorrow and that would be one more, infinitesimal bereavement. Tomorrow she would go through one more separation from Graham—the meeting with him would be no more than a preparation for the inevitable breach. She closed the flap carefully, knowing now what was underneath. A section of her was composed of the ability, the necessity to part; the inevitability of parting. She must always beware. Nothing would ever be permanent.

Partly out of deference to the disappointed manager, and partly because she was impatient with this image she had discovered, she changed into a black trouser suit with a great gold chain, like an insignia, round her neck. She went down to the lounge and ordered a vodka and tonic and read yet another copy of *Country Life*.

'Excuse me, ma'am. I think we've met over at the school. My name's Pepper, Max Pepper.'

She looked up, astounded. He was a stocky man with curling grey hair and the heightened colour of someone who has been drinking for thirty years.

'May I sit down?'

'Of course.'

'I think you're Mrs. Strathearn, young Philip's mother?' She nodded.

'I knew it. My boy's in the same class. I saw you at Parents' Day last summer. You were wearing a blue dress with a sort of . . .' His large hands clumsily sketched some sort of frill round his neck. 'He told me you were Philip's mother. I said lucky Philip. Believe me. That's what I said. Lucky Philip.' He laughed with extraordinary noise. She was surprised that the two other couples in the lounge did not turn and stare.

She did not have to ask any questions, or indeed make any comment. He went on, leaning towards her, his elbows on his knees, his head cocked sideways. 'Russell—that's my boy —has been getting into a bit of trouble. That's why I'm down here. Sorting it out. It seems he concocted some sort of cigarette and sold it as hash. Can you believe that?' Again the great laugh roared out. 'Sold it as hash! They were going to send him home for a week, but I talked them out of that. I'm a bachelor father, you see. My wife went off a couple of years ago. The only time I hear from her is when the money's not on time. If Russell came home he'd probably be on hash all day, God knows there's plenty in the apartment if he knows where to look for it. Hey, what are you drinking?'

She said vodka and tonic. The fact that the waiter took so long to come seemed to unnerve him. He snapped his fingers, bringing the young Italian reluctantly to his side. 'Vodka and tonic for the lady. And a scotch on the rocks.'

The waiter gave a little bow, looking at Eleanor. She tried to say with her eyes, 'I can't help it.'

'So what do you think of the school, eh? I think it's fantastic. They've got discipline, you know. Back in the States, there'd be no discipline in a school like that. I don't live in the States, by the way. Haven't done for fifteen years. I have an apartment off Charles Street. I'm in the film business, by the way. Same thing nowadays as saying you're a pauper.'

She expected the laugh and narrowed her eyes to shut out the sound.

'Where do you live?'

'St. John's Wood.'

'Oh yes. They've got a new American school up there now. I thought of it for Russell, but it's no good the boy being home without a mother. He'll be making my secretary before long, by the look of him. You married?'

She hesitated. 'Separated.'

'That's right. Who isn't. Who ever heard of a happily married couple in 1971? I've got a girl, but I don't take much account of her. Always moaning. I hate moaners. You and I should get together, go to the theatre a bit and so on. Do you like the theatre?'

'Sometimes.'

'Ah, I can see you're bright. I like a bright woman. You know you might think, from the look of me, that I'm the sort who'd go for the dolly birds. I'm not. I like a good, bright, funny, sexy woman. Like you.'

She had to join in his laughter. There was something endearing in the fact that he was so shameless. The two vodkas had eased her. She asked tentatively, 'What do you do ... in the film business?'

'Oh, I produce ... write a few scripts.' In fact, in his world, he was very well known, but her ignorance pleased him. 'Let's not talk about me. How about dinner?'

'You have to have it in the bar if you're not going to the dinner-dance. It's not terribly comfortable.'

'Then let's go to the dinner-dance. I can still do a fairly respectable chassis. What's your first name, by the way?'

'Eleanor.'

'Well, Nell, let's rock 'em with a touch of the Gene Kellys.'

She had begun to giggle inside; soon it would come out. The head waiter, hardly raising his eyebrows, led them to a table on the edge of the dance floor. Pepper walked like a sailor; he was not bulky, but square, strong and, she felt certain, extremely hairy. He ordered champagne. 'Usually I hate this place. Don't like being on my own, no one to talk to. Let's celebrate.'

She gathered, from the endless stream of information that flowed across the table, that he was a genuinely concerned father, inordinately proud of his son, only waiting for the day when he could take him around, show him a good time. He visited him often.

'What d'you say we all have lunch tomorrow, the four of us?'

'Not possible, I'm afraid. My husband's coming down.'

'So it's that sort of separation? You're still carrying the torch for him, eh?'

'No,' she said, and almost believed it. 'But we get together to see Philip sometimes.'

'And what about the vacations?'

'I don't really know. We haven't had one yet, I mean since . . . I think Philip and I may go to Greece.'

'Then you don't mind about the Colonels?'

'Yes. But I don't see why they should make Philip lose . . . thousands of years of civilisation. I don't see why he should suffer.'

'Not only bright,' he said, 'but bloody-minded as well. It could be you're my ideal woman.'

'Thank you,' she said. They toasted each other with the sweet champagne. Before they had got through the hors-d'œuvres she had learned most of the salient facts about his two marriages, the fact that he had a house on the Costa del Sol ('Right near Marbella. Why don't you bring the boy to stay?') and a flat in St. Moritz.

'Russell's a champion skier. Does your boy ski?'

'No.'

'Then he should learn. Bring him out next Christmas, I'll find him a good teacher. And I'll give you private lessons.'

This, she supposed, with another inward explosion of laughter, was the kind of man who was suitable for a middle-aged woman like yourself: unattached, rich, generous, tolerant, a good father. But oh, she said, misting over with champagne, how I long for Kilcannon. The burly, noisy man opposite her became, momentarily, elegant and sardonic, disdainful of the sugary drink, his hand open to receive hers.

'Do you have a fellow at the moment?' Pepper was asking.

'No,' she laughed. 'I'm in what you might call no-man's land.'

'I don't believe it. But that's good.'

The band had been making lengthy preparations, twanging and drumming and leafing through sheets of music. Now, with concerted zest, they burst into 'Hullo, Dolly'.

'Come on,' Pepper said. 'Let's show 'em.'

She was reluctant, but he had hauled her to her feet before she could say a word. He turned out to be a nifty dancer, content to jump and twirl on his own while she slowly felt the artless music reach her feet and then waded in further, knees and hips and shoulders, almost forgetting Pepper, rediscovering the part of her that was Jessica and free and blameless. When the music stopped there was a sparse scattering of applause; she realised with amazement that it was not for the band, but for herself and the extraordinary Pepper.

'Well,' he said, panting, 'you're a dancer as well. How many more secrets have you got tucked away in that pretty head of yours?'

'Plenty.'

'Listen,' he said, bringing out a neat address book with M.P. inscribed in gold on the cover, 'I must have your phone number.'

She gave it to him.

'And your address?'

She gave it to him.

'Good. Now we're friends. Are we friends?'

'Yes,' she said, smiling.

'And we'll go to a few shows and take in a bit of swinging London?'

She swallowed, pressing her tongue to the roof of her mouth so that only the right, the advisable, word might come out.

'Yes.'

The band had started 'Moon River'.

'Ah,' he said, 'my tune.'

This time he held her against the hard bulge of his stomach and his hand was hot on the small of her back. Worse, he sang, groaning into her left ear, his whisky breath damp on her neck.

'You're a lovely lady,' he said, 'and this is the best evening I've had in months.'

'I'm glad.' She really was happy that for some reason she made him happy.

Somehow, in the intervals of dancing, they got through the fleshless duck à l'orange with frozen sprouts. They had more champagne. They had brandy. In the middle of some moaning tune from *My Fair Lady* he kissed her, his mouth unexpectedly soft, his tongue sliding between her teeth.

'Just to show we're friends,' he said, and grinned, rather shamefaced like a small boy who has just used a swear word. It was the first time she had been kissed—except, remotely, by Graham—since her meeting with Kilcannon. She took it like a woman, with grace, aptitude, and a gradual, but firm, withdrawal. Her mouth felt at the same time eager and disgusted. She realised that he was planning to sleep with her and her merriment dwindled and failed. His face was blotched with drink, and he was no longer speaking, but shouting. The idea of being touched by him was repellent, however great her need. She gathered herself together.

'I'm going to bed now. Thank you for the evening.'

He looked at her almost quizzically, and kept his voice down.

'Can I come?'

'No?' But some weakness in her, some need not to reject or be rejected, made her add, 'Not tonight.'

'But you're going back to town tomorrow?'

'Yes.'

He shrugged it off, a man used to minor disappointments. 'O.K., then. But I'll see you in London?'

She smiled. 'I'll see you tomorrow.'

'Yes. But your husband will be here. I'll see you in London.'

'All right.'

She kissed him briefly, for giving her a good time, and left him ordering another brandy, the restaurant almost empty, the band packed up and gone away. She knew—God, she knew—how lonely he was. She looked at herself in the mirror in the lift and thought, Oh, knight, sweet knight, why aren't you with me? Her mouth twitched down at the corners in a self-critical, self-ridiculing smile. What malicious fate had provided her with Max Pepper? Perhaps she should go to Marbella, drink gin fizzes under parasols and sleep with him, sweating among the mosquitoes? Of course you should, Graham said: take life as you find it.

'Those gigantic rocks with monasteries on the top, I like the sound of Meteora . . .'

The smile widened, she put her hand over her reflection in the mirror as though keeping a secret.

13

In her soft, silk-covered bed she had her recurring dream of being in the old, the original, house, which was decomposing, floors rotting, ceilings collapsing, unmanageable chaos everywhere. She couldn't make up her quarrel with Graham *because he wasn't there*—a total conviction of his absence. And yet he was there, telephoning in the bedroom and saying 'Hullo, sexy' to someone on the other end of the line. He said that he wasn't capable of making love to her, Eleanor. She said (knowing it wasn't true) that she didn't mind, she just wanted to love him. And she knew he was lying, because his face, so much younger than his real face, was smiling.

In her dream Philip, as a small child, woke up at 3.30 a.m. She tried to get him back to bed, but Graham sat down on the landing with him to play slums. 'We just have to set out this slum,' he said, and they had a board with little lead figures, like the Peter Rabbit game of her childhood. She wandered about the house looking for signs of Graham, of his infidelities, but there were none. There was a water tank in the attic on which was painted the word 'Gravesend'.

Eating her breakfast, which was wheeled in on a trolley by the same, but now white-coated, Italian, she puzzled over the dream for a little and then forgot it. Gravesend presumably had something to do with Graves Avenue, the name of her street: graves, tombs, vaults, catacombs, sepulchres and houses of death. The game of slums was an enigma, unless a slum was the state of her house: the state of her mind? The sun was shining, the toast thin and soft, the coffee quite tolerable. She telephoned Graham, supported by the soft pillows and looking out over the ruffled lake.

He was woken up by the phone, his voice growling with sleep.

'Can you come a bit earlier, and pick up Philip?'

'Can I what?'

'Come a bit earlier and pick up Philip.'

'Why?'

'Because he wants you to. He wants to show off the Porsche.'

'What's the time now?'

'Nine o'clock.'

'What time do I have to be there?'

'It doesn't matter. About eleven.'

An enormous yawn, which must, surely, wake Nell Partwhistle.

'All right. See you about eleven-thirty.'

'All right.'

It was perfectly so: he wasn't there. A voice spoke, a body would arrive, but he would not be there. He was absent, and had always been absent. Not unlike Kilcannon. She remembered Max Pepper and wondered, with dread, whether he would be up and about. She read the Sunday papers; that is, she dabbled in them, pecked at them like someone with no appetite. Women, it seemed, were still learning how to be perfect women; men were still recounting the trivia of their domestic lives, ordering further bombing of countries from which they had technically withdrawn, battling to save the Welsh language from extinction; both were pronouncing, with varying degrees of wit and readability, on films, plays, books and television programmes which nobody who had not seen that film, play, television programme, or read that particular book, cared about. They were the week's dose of depression, and resulted in a distraught, papery mess of garbage. She scooped them all up and crammed them into the tiny, decorated waste-paper basket. Then she took a long time bathing and dressing, making up her face to look naked and her lips to look lip-coloured. As she stood at the window she saw Max Pepper, dressed in a kind of safari outfit, walking across the car park to his car, which was immense and electric blue and American and would put the Porsche to shame. He unlocked it, got in, switched on the engine and with only the faintest of purrs was away; to fetch Russell, presumably, and give him a good time.

When Philip arrived with Graham he seemed once again the familiar, silent person, loaded with worries or dreams. Graham, who was getting very fat, was dressed for the country in a silk choker, suède jacket and, of all things, denim trousers. The boy went off to the lavatory, and Graham asked belligerently, 'What the hell's the matter with him? What have you been saying to him?'

She answered calmly, 'As far as I know there's nothing the matter with him. And I haven't been saying anything to him. Why?'

'He won't speak.'

'That's not very unusual.' But she remembered, with pleasure, their walk round the lake.

'You're turning him against me. That's obvious.'

'Don't be ridiculous.'

'Then why won't he talk to me?'

'Perhaps he hasn't got anything to say.'

'He says you're going to Greece in the holidays.'

'Yes. He says you're going to Portugal.'

'Well, I'm bloody well going to have him to stay in Portugal.'

'Of course you are.' She put her hand over his, a kind of re-dreaming of her dream. 'It's all right. Don't be so angry. It's all right.'

He went off, he said, to telephone his Answering Service. Philip returned and told her, with difficulty, that they had had a dance last night, not bad. She told him about her dinner with Max Pepper.

'Oh God,' he said, 'Russell's the end. He's a Fascist.'

'What d'you mean?'

'Well . . . you know . . . he's plastic.'

'His father seems very fond of him.'

'It's a good thing someone is.'

'Are you . . . angry about something?'

'When you've been for a few hours in that bloody school you get angry.'

'Why?'

He heaved his whole body as though in extreme discomfort. 'I don't know. You just do.'

Graham came back more cheerful and they drank Bloody Marys, Philip had draught bitter. They were a family. Graham told some amusing, though to Eleanor indiscreet, stories about his patients. Philip laughed with a single sound: 'Huh.' Max Pepper and Russell, a large, handsome boy, came and sat at the other end of the lounge. As far as Eleanor could see they were both drinking whisky. Russell seemed to be talking incessantly, and his father frequently laughed that deafening laugh, making Philip flinch and huddle into his beer.

'Who in God's name is that ghastly fellow?' Graham asked.

'He's Max Pepper. I had dinner with him last night.'

'That must have been charming for you.'

'Yes,' she said. 'In a way it was. Russell's in Philip's class.'

'Worse luck,' muttered Philip.

They were a family, but they had no common ground. Not one of them really knew how the other two lived. Philip, released a little by the beer, told them that the mother of one of his friends had committed suicide by throwing herself out of her bedroom window. Eleanor was shocked, horrified by the implied pain and loss, by the effect, however distant, on Philip.

'When I was young,' Graham said, 'my professor in psychiatry gave me an old man to look after. You can imagine I was pretty chuffed, I mean my first patient and all that. The old fellow had thrombosis and a cardiac disease and a perforated bowel, he could hardly stand up. Anyway, he was also extremely depressed, which wasn't surprising, and kept on babbling about throwing himself out of windows. So they had him in this hospital, six floors up, and they watched the old fool night and day. One evening he conned the nurses into leaving him alone for two minutes. I swear, two minutes. During that time he heaved himself off a bed that was four feet off the ground, climbed over a chest of drawers and a couple of chairs, got himself up on to the window-sill, unscrewed the windows, opened them, and behold—no old fellow, only a nasty mess on the ground six floors down.'

This uproarious story was greeted with utter silence, except for Graham's reminiscent chuckle. Philip finished his beer and suggested that they went in to lunch. He passed Russell without a glance, but Eleanor, following Graham, received a huge wink from Max and a curious thumbs-up sign which was perhaps meant to give her courage.

Philip was less voracious today, and mumbled his order for avocado pear and grilled sole. Without looking at the wine list, Graham commanded a bottle of Chablis to come immediately. He called the New Zealand waitress 'darling', which sent her into such a flutter that she had to come back twice to make sure she had got the orders right.

'So,' Graham said. 'Shall I tell you about Portugal?'

'All right,' Philip said.

'Well. It overlooks the sea and it's got three acres of gardens, presumably looked after by some Portuguese, and it's got a huge verandah with vines . . .'

Using some extraordinary inner machinery, Eleanor closed her ears. They had gone abroad every summer—even last summer—to Italy, Spain, France, Greece, Morocco. One surprising August they had even been to Kenya and Tanzania, Daphne and Jessica and Philip bobbing about in the back of a jeep with their Instamatics at the ready, great red elephants looming out of the dust. As far as Graham was concerned, his patients could be committed, or slit their throats, or even recover, during the month of August. He had a locum, a mild and efficient doctor who was more at ease with physical diseases than he was with emotional disturbances. Graham went on holiday. Most years they had taken houses, some very like the one he was now—soundlessly, as far as Eleanor was concerned—describing. They had made love in Grasse and Fez and Thebes and Sorrento, and in a tent where they could hear the lions yawning in the brushwood. She could not bear the insensitivity, the apparent lack of feeling, with which he was describing this place from which she was barred, this place where the faceless Nell Partwhistle would walk about in her bikini, breathing in love with the sun. She was almost angry, her toes clenched inside her shoes, her hand holding the wineglass as though it were made of iron.

'. . . and there's a boat,' Graham was saying, 'so we'll take it out and go for picnics . . .'

'Great,' Philip said. 'When shall I come?'

'Well, it depends when you'll be back from this . . . Greek trip.'

'We're only going for a couple of weeks.'

'Then directly you get back. I'll get Trixie to fix it all up. We're going to drive there, it should be fun.'

'We', the intolerable, abominable 'we'. She was afraid she was going to cry, which would be inexcusable. But what else could they talk about? Could she tell them about Cressida and Ellis about Daphne's new lover . . .

'I think Daphne's going to get married,' she said quickly, like someone who knows the words before they have turned the page.

'Married?' Graham ridiculed the idea. 'Who to?'

130

'His name's Hereward.'

'Good God,' Graham said, but Philip giggled.

'Has he got any money?'

'Yes, I think so. A bit. He does something with pop music.'

'What?' Philip asked, interested.

'I don't know. You'll have to ask him. Anyway, he's moved in to Daphne's flat and she says they plan to get married in July.'

'Does Hereward,' Graham asked, 'know about this?'

She smiled. For a moment they were the couple who had laughed at things other people didn't understand, and remained glum while other people were splitting their sides.

'I don't know.'

'Perhaps he ought to be told.'

'He will be,' Philip said. 'By Daphne.'

'I suppose she'll have to have a wedding and all that,' Graham said. 'Though God knows why. Why, actually, are they getting married?'

'She says she's tired of having affairs,' Eleanor said.

'And what about Hereward? Is he a pouf or something?'

'They run in the family,' Philip said, and drank some of Graham's wine.

Drugged with the wine—they had got through two bottles —Eleanor slept while Graham and Philip played ping-pong and draughts and walked sternly, without much conversation, round the lake. Graham said he had an appointment at five, and must go. He appeared in Eleanor's bedroom and woke her up, flushed and rumpled.

'I've got to go.'

'Oh . . . all right.' She got off the bed, as though it were somehow indecent to be seen there, and walked in her stockinged feet to the dressing table to brush her hair.

'I wish we could be friendly,' Graham said.

'But we are friendly.'

'I wish you'd come round and . . . meet Nell or something. It'd make her feel much better.'

She stared at him. 'Would it really?'

'Of course. I mean, we have to be civilised about this. There's no point in all this . . . enmity.'

'There isn't any enmity.'

'Well. There's something.'

'Could it be guilt?'

'I'm not in the slightest degree guilty about anything.'

'Good.' She held her head on one side as she brushed out her hair. 'How are Crookston, Push and Mandeville coming along?'

'Slowly. You make such impossible demands.'

'I don't. Rothman, Bich and Bite do. Particularly Bite.'

'Well . . . we'll arrange something.' He came over as though to kiss her. 'Goodbye, Nell.'

'I'm not Nell,' she said unworthily. 'I'm Eleanor.'

'Then goodbye, Eleanor.' He kissed both her cheeks while she held the hairbrush awkwardly. 'See you soon.'

'Yes . . .'

She watched him go and close the door, and heard him walk down the corridor. Then grief hit her like a tidal wave, she was knocked flat on the bed, drowned, submerged, uselessly fighting, uselessly crying, 'Oh Graham . . . Graham . . . Graham . . .' The silk eiderdown was drenched and smeared. She thought of running after him and pleading, Take me with you, take me home. She heard a car engine start up outside and ran to the window, her fists clenched as though to beat on it. The yellow Porsche backed and turned and shot away down the road. She sat down on the dressing-table stool. A ballet dancer could not have more perfectly expressed physical misery; her whole body was spineless, drooped in total despair. There was a timid knock on the door.

'Yes?' She reached for a tissue to hide her face.

'It's only me. Are you awake?'

'Yes, I'm awake.' She kept her head turned away. 'And it's time for tea.'

Philip loafed about the room while she repaired her face.

He knew perfectly well that she had been crying, and why, and his inability to do anything about it, even to comfort her, locked every word in his head.

'That's a pretty ghastly car Pepper's got.'

'I thought you'd think it was . . . rather impressive.'

'No. It's plastic.'

Five minutes later she said, 'Come on, then. Let's have an enormous tea.'

She found that Graham had paid her bill, even to the enormous tea they were eating while he sped, radio blaring, to London. She packed, Philip took her suitcase out to the car, they embarked on another parting.

'It'll be nice in Greece,' he said as they drove.

'Yes. I'm looking forward to it.'

'What will you do while I'm in Portugal?'

'I don't know.' Inspiration struck her. 'I'll probably go down and stay with Grandmother Bennet.'

'She sent me a chocolate cake. It was delicious.'

'Did you write and thank her?'

'No. I haven't had time.'

'Then you must,' she said sternly, 'write and thank her.'

'All right,' he sighed. 'I will.'

The school again, the children assembling after their long, and possibly difficult, Sundays. He got out of the car quickly; the only way to deal with emotion was to whip yourself through it as though through a candle-flame; to grasp it so swiftly and so hard that you didn't feel the pain.

'Goodbye, then. See you soon.'

'Yes. And *write*.'

'I will,' he lied.

For once, he stood waiting for her to go. When she had turned he raised his hand in a kind of salute. She felt so much pain that she was unconscious of most of the drive and only became aware when she was already in the outskirts of London. Would Cressida be there? If she wasn't, if the house was dark and empty, a house of death, where could she go?

To Jessica, perhaps? To Daphne and Hereward? Both of these were perfectly reasonable possibilities. Both Jessica and Daphne would have taken her in with love and understanding. But she was not yet capable of comprehending that her daughters could be perfectly competent mothers. Only Cressida was allowed to see that she could often be a child in need of care; and even there she felt guilty, as though she was in some way letting Cressida down. In her own way she was repeating the pattern of herself and Mrs. Bennet: depriving her children of responsibility, lying to them by making out that she was resistant and self-governing, limiting their ability to feel and to act freely from their feelings. She thought that she was encouraging their independence, but by her remoteness, her brave face, the no-nonsense voice she put on when her heart was breaking, she bound them to her by worry and uneasiness and, worst, the suspicion that she was being dishonest with them. These were flaps still to be opened. At the moment she felt that if Cressida were not there she would simply, immediately, like a light being put out, die.

But Ellis's car was outside. The sitting-room curtains were drawn, the windows glowed. Thank God, she said out loud; and, as one does in moments of extreme stress, meant it.

14

'So we're going to get married,' Daphne said. It was Sunday, and she was propped up in bed with her hands folded across her stomach, her hair half drawn like a curtain, to let in a little light.

'If you want to,' Hereward said. He had a slight Cockney accent because he was of the generation that in its teens had venerated Michael Caine. At the moment he was carefully arranging the breakfast, which he had cooked, around Daphne. She took a cup of tea and held it under her chin.

'Church or register office?'

'Oh, blimey, I don't know. Register office.'

'Which one?'

'Whichever one'll have us. Eat your eggs.'

'Hampstead. Yes, I think Hampstead. I mean, we could go to Chelsea, but that'd mean putting a suitcase there for six weeks or something, wouldn't it?'

'How should I know? I never got married before.'

'And what about the reception?'

'The what?'

'You know. The party, for relatives and everything. All your trendy friends.'

'Why don't we just have a party? Loads of drink and loads of hash and lots of lovely dollies.'

'I'm talking,' Daphne said with dignity, 'about our wedding reception. We'll have to have the grandmothers and people like that.'

'Oh Gawd, you've never met my grandma. She'd scare the parson out of his wits.'

'You don't have a parson. You have a registrar. Sometimes I believe they're women.'

'Don't tell me,' he said, 'I'm going to be married by a bloody woman. That I will not take.'

She loved him, stretching out her hand and putting it flat against his chest. 'I'll see to it.'

'You'd better. Being married by a bloody woman . . .'

'We could have the reception at Mum's house. Dad has to pay, anyway. Should we,' she was immensely serious, 'have a cake?'

'What for?'

'A wedding cake is usual.'

He rolled on to the bed, taking her cup and saucer away from her and almost tumbling her on to the breakfast tray. 'I love you,' he said. 'God, I love you.'

They kissed and wrestled for a few minutes. Then she gently pushed him away and composed herself. 'Well? Should we?'

'Should we what?'

'Have a wedding cake?'

'Have a bloody roast ox for all I care. By the way, when is this ceremony going to be?'

'Well. Mum's going to Greece with Philip on August 4th. And Philip breaks up on July 19th. And our friendly neighbourhood genius is going away for his hols on July 21st.'

'Where's he going to?' Hereward was fascinated by Daphne's employer, who seemed to live a life of ease and luxury from doing absolutely nothing.

'He's booked in in Sardinia, Antigua, Miami Beach and Monkton Combe, Somerset. He'll probably decide about ten o'clock at night on July 20th. It'll be a nasty day.'

'And what will make him decide?'

'Whichever bird happens to be available. Or maybe he'll meet one on July 19th. God knows he tries hard enough.'

'I'm never going to believe he hasn't tried it on you.'

'Well, he hasn't. Or I haven't let him. How about August 2nd?'

'What, I ask myself, is wrong with August 2nd?'

'I wish you'd take it seriously. After all, we are getting married.'

'For better or for worse?'

Her mouth dropped, she turned her head away.

'Look,' he said, 'I know you want a lovely wedding and a lovely party and a lovely cake, and August 2nd is a lovely day. As far as I'm concerned it doesn't matter a damn because I love you. Take over, baby. Do exactly what you want. If there are any bills, I'll sign them.'

He stalked off to have his bath. Daphne lay limp, her chin on her chest. Two-thirds of her was fear; one-third perked a bright head above water and prattled on about wedding cakes and receptions and God knows what. All she wanted was Hereward, his body and his convoluted, warm heart. She wanted to care for him and bathe him in her care for ever. Something about marriage, the solemnity it should have, and its element of sacrifice, was necessary to her. She barely remembered days, months, even years with her father when she was the favoured one, Cressida and Marcus awkward and old, Jessica not yet born. Daphne, so pretty and cute, had been taken to Harrods every Saturday morning and been given knickerbocker glories in the Silver Grill. Daphne had been taken riding before she was half as high as a pony, and had once, by some dramatic tearaway on the part of her horse, been had up for speeding in Richmond Park. Daphne had been given U.S. Cavalry forts and Indian encampments, made by Graham out of plywood and plaster and paint in the days when he was still home in the evenings. Daphne had been told stories and had been read to, and had blown open the silver door of her father's watch, and had been taught two-handed whist, and had curled up against the still young chest, smelling a curious mixture of sweat, cologne and anaesthetic. Daphne had been the favourite. And then suddenly, it seemed, without warning, she was being shouted and snarled at; she hid her breasts behind folded arms, and shrouded her hips in gym slips; her beautiful little face became frightened, she grew her hair like a blind. Somewhere below her, Jessica and Philip were getting some attention; though never as much as she had had. She ran away. Her love for her father had grown rather than lessened; he was her faithless lover, infatuation unrequited, trust betrayed. Until Hereward she had never found a substitute. And even this substitute she felt was a sham. Tears ran like glycerine from under her long lashes. It's all so hopeless, she thought. He'll never understand.

Hereward was aware—he could hardly fail to be—of Daphne's sudden plunges into despair, but he was too shrewd, too downright sensible, to dismiss them as 'moods'. He understood why she wanted to get married, and he understood why he did not (very much) want to get married. Of the two, her argument and need seemed the more urgent. He did understand, but knew that it would probably take years of patience before she believed that he did. He was twenty-three, and prepared for years of patience. His own mother and father, who owned what he called a stripped-pine boutique at the World's End, were devoted to each other: over fifty, and he swore they made love every night. He was used to a life in which sex was demonstrable and tolerance, compassion and simple affection predominated. It was therefore curiously easy for him to take on Daphne with her ups and downs, her buried sense of betrayal, her tendency to martyrdom and her damnable efficiency. He had had plenty of girls, but none who interested him as much as Daphne. The rest of the family, those he had met, were all right too. Cressida was a bit sombre, and Eleanor needed a fellow, but he thoroughly approved of Jessica and her boy. He looked forward to meeting Philip and, most of all, Marcus. To have the courage to be a queer when you were the eldest of that *galère* was really something. He splashed himself liberally with cologne and deodorant and after-shave and padded back into the bedroom smelling like a posy.

'All right,' Daphne said. 'We won't get married.'

'All right,' he said. 'We won't.'

'But I want to!'

He sat down naked on the edge of the bed.

'Shut up,' he said, 'or I'll give you a good hiding.'

Drowned in hair, her watery smile was invisible.

'D'you want to know what we're going to do?'

She nodded.

'We're going to get up and go down Petticoat Lane and buy something. Then we're going to have an enormous lunch at Polly's. Then we're going to come back here and have a stupendous fuck and go to sleep. This evening I shall watch television and you, undoubtedly, will do your washing. That brings us one day nearer to August 2nd. Are you with me so far?'

She nodded.

'We will get invitations printed and open a wedding list at . . . I don't know, Habitat or Heal's or Marks and Sparks. That makes sure that everyone gives us toast racks and tea-makers and things we can flog. We will approach your mum about having the party at her house, and your dad about paying for it all. I'll tell my own mum and dad that the one thing we don't want is stripped-pine furniture. Then you'll buy a staggering dress.'

She pushed back her hair, as interested now as when Graham used to tell her about Black Duke Michael.

'White, I think, and extremely simple, but extraordinarily expensive. Then we'll go to this registrar fellow and publish the banns or whatever we have to do, and book the theatre. Right? We'll get a firm of caterers to do the party and when it's all over we'll come back here and get stoned. *Now* do you want to get married?'

Foolishly, she was now crying much harder than when she had been unhappy. She pulled him down into her damp hair, he kissed her streaming eyes and sticky cheeks but would not make love to her.

'We stick to our plan,' he said. 'Up and out.'

She put out her tongue at him and he chased her into the bath, where he washed her back with vigorous tenderness.

15

The weather was hot, day after day of gritty, grinding sunshine. Cressida bought a number of ankle-length cotton dresses, Quaker grey and faded blue and fern green, and walked from Eleanor's house to Ellis's studio with her hair tied smoothly back, angry, beautiful, dressed for milking some eighteenth-century cow.

She *was* angry. Ellis was at the peak of his indecision about whether he wanted Gwen, or Cressida, or both, or neither. Gwen would be home in another ten days. She had written many loving letters. Compared with Gwen, God had a mean streak in forgiveness. As for Cressida, she loved Tom McGraw, but it was like loving in a dream and every time Ellis bundled her into his arms she felt both the relief and disappointment of waking up. He kept her up all night, not making love but interminably discussing, interminably arguing the pros and cons of some non-existent dilemma. She was worn out and furious about getting herself into yet another sterile, futureless situation. She did not discuss it with Eleanor, because that would be in some way obscene, almost incestuous. She did not discuss it with Daphne, because Daphne disapproved of the whole thing and was in any case too full of her own concerns. Oddly enough, the only person she could really have talked to was Tom McGraw, and he was in Virginia. She might have moved in with Ellis, which would have been some sort of statement, but the commitment was too much for either of them. Ellis insisted that he loved her, adored her, but some hard, undamaged organ inside him, the isolated strong-room of his independence where the alcohol never reached, resisted her; as, indeed, it resisted everyone. He had to be alone, and he had to hate it. Cressida wanted to go and stay with Grandmother Bennet, the only person who did not make her angry, but the situation held her fast; the walls were nearly reaching the sky.

In preparation for the wedding, and with complete disregard for her dwindling resources, Eleanor had engaged a firm to make her an instant garden. Toiling in the sun, three shirtless youths laid turf and brick paths, heaved great sacks of soil and compost; later, three older men, with the absent gaze and pitted fingernails of gardeners, came and planted shrubs and roses in disposable pots which, like buried flesh, disintegrated. She had lavender and puny creepers and a pot of herbs and a number of plants whose names sounded like something out of Graham's medical dictionary. 'We have diagnosed', she wrote to Philip, 'a severe case of venidio-arctotis, but are still suffering from eucomis comosa . . .' When it was all finished, and the spray playing over the new slabs of turf, she enjoyed it, though with a feeling of guilt. Mrs. Bennet would have done all this herself, though she might reluctantly have allowed a man to come and do the bricklaying. She wondered, as she pulled out the fast-growing weeds and put them in a plastic bag, whether Mrs. Bennet was actually a woman, or a man in woman's flesh. Mrs. Bennet had always disliked and feared sex so much that it was impossible to tell what she might have been if her true feelings had ever been revealed. A good husband? How could a woman be a good husband? Just as easily as Marcus, from all she heard, was a good wife. Then what about her father, the mild-mannered man with brown blotches on the backs of his hand like some gentle animal? He had farmed his farm in a gentlemanly way, and kept the peace, but at home he had been submissive, painting a few small water-colours, tinkling a little on the piano, teaching them to play Up-Jenkins and Hunt the Thimble—an admirable, if ineffective, wife. And she herself, Eleanor . . . what was she? Both and neither. Nothing. She stuffed the plastic bag in the dustbin and realised why gardeners had such a distant look: they were concerned with thinking.

Mrs. Strathearn came to tea to meet Hereward. They had tea on the new patio outside Philip's room, on a real garden table with real garden chairs. Mrs. Strathearn, Eleanor, Daphne and Hereward sat at the table; Cressida and Jessica on the lawn, with Juniper pissing on the grass which, since she was a bitch, would rapidly come out in neat bleached patches. Mrs. Strathearn liked Hereward for his easy manners, which she imagined had been learned at some public school; Mrs. Bennet could not get over his accent, though she said she was sure he was a nice boy at heart.

'But won't the reception cost a great deal?' Mrs. Strathearn asked, thinking of Graham.

'Not really,' Hereward said. 'I know a fellow who can get us champagne at cost price. We needn't have much nosh.'

Mrs. Strathearn looked enquiring.

'Food,' Daphne said.

'Oh. But a cake, of course?'

'Naturally.'

'And where will you go for your honeymoon?'

'Nowhere,' Hereward said.

'We'd rather stay at home,' Daphne said.

'I see.' She accepted their curious ways because they did not really affect her; she did not feel one way or the other about Daphne's honeymoon, or, if the truth were told, about her wedding. Of course she hoped the child would be happy; unhappiness, like bad manners, was simply not done.

'And have you,' she asked Hereward, 'met Daphne's father?'

143

'Graham? No, we're going to have dinner with them next week.'

'Juniper!' Eleanor snapped. 'Get out of the lavender!'

'She's not doing it any harm.' Jessica held the puppy as though the lavender had attacked it.

'Where's Brian?' Cressida asked.

'He's working. How's Ellis?' Jessica was the only one of the family who accepted Ellis as a matter of course, though she could not stay in the same room with him when he was drunk.

'Confused.'

Mrs. Strathearn listened to this family chat with an expression of deaf interest. In truth, she did not understand it, but that did not worry her. Mrs. Bennet would have been asking (in the unlikely event that she did not already know), 'Who's Brian? . . . Who's Ellis? . . . What's he working at? . . . Why is he confused?' Mrs. Strathearn said tranquilly, 'Your garden is very pretty, dear. Did it cost a great deal?'

'No,' Eleanor lied. 'It was quite reasonable.'

'It must be nice for you to be able to sit out.'

'Yes,' Eleanor said. 'It is.'

'It's such a pity that Graham only has that little balcony. It's too small even to put a chair out.'

'I know,' Eleanor said.

'And do you know he's invited me to Portugal? I shan't go, of course.'

'Why not?' Jessica asked. 'Of course you must go.'

'Yes,' Daphne said. 'Of course you must.'

'Of course you must go,' Cressida said.

Mrs. Strathearn was rather surprised, and touched, by the chorus. They were really very nice girls. She smiled at them, demanding more.

'I'm far too old. All that way . . .'

'Of course you're not!'

'All you have to do is sit in an aeroplane . . .'

'And Dad'll meet you . . .'

144

'It's easier,' Jessica said, as though she had been comparing the distances, 'than going to Cornwall.'

'Well . . . it would certainly be very pleasant. And when is Philip going?'

'About August 18th,' Eleanor said, stacking the crumby plates. Daphne immediately got up to help her.

'No, you stay here and talk. Cressida will help.'

Always bloody Cressida, Cressida thought. It was not the clearing away, the washing up, that enraged her. It was partly the fuss that Daphne seemed to be making about her wedding, but more, much more, her own infertility. While they were washing up, Eleanor suddenly put her arm round her and held her tightly.

'Tom is missing you,' she said. 'Really he is.'

'I know.'

'There's nothing to stop you having a baby if you want to. You'll never exactly get his permission.'

'It would be a cheat,' Cressida said.

'It might make him happy.'

'Yes. I think it would.'

'Then why not cheat a little? Perhaps he just doesn't know what's good for him.'

'I can't,' Cressida said. 'Not with Tom.'

She didn't know what made her say it. 'Or with Ellis?'

'You're not serious?'

'No.'

'I'm not taking the pill,' Cressida said. 'And nothing's happened.'

'Does Ellis know that?'

'No.'

'Then you *are* cheating him—I mean, according to you— aren't you?

'Oh, I don't know!' Cressida cried. 'I don't bloody know!'

For once Eleanor was severe, although afterwards she wondered about her motive. 'You must go to a doctor immediately. You can go to Henderson, he'll give you a prescription. But immediately. Like today. You know perfectly well Gwen's coming home. You know perfectly well she'll move back in with him.'

'Why do you always take her side?' Cressida blazed. 'It' me you should be thinking of! Or are you—perhaps you're thinking of yourself!'

'Cressie—for God's sake ...'

'You don't help me! You just criticise! If I want to go back on the pill, it's my business, not yours!'

'I know,' Eleanor said, shaking.

'Then don't give me your bloody advice! It's me who's having an affair with Ellis, not you! Just leave me alone!'

She ran out of the kitchen and the front door slammed. Eleanor leant on the sink, breathing in great gulps of air.

'I must be off,' Mrs. Strathearn said, popping her head round the kitchen door in order not to be involved with the washing up. 'It was so nice meeting Hereward ... and seeing all the children.'

Eleanor swallowed hard. It was like swallowing an entire heart in one gulp. She turned, blinking as though the sunlight were too strong.

'Must you go?'

'My car will be waiting. He is always very punctual, and I told him to be here exactly at five o'clock. I'm afraid it's five past. It was so nice to see you, dear.' She proffered a shy cheek. 'Where's Cressie?'

'She ... she had to go out. She asked me to say goodbye.'

'Do come round and see me. Any time.'

'Yes, I will.'

She walked to the door and saw the old lady into her waiting car. The street was empty, all the schoolchildren gone home, the office workers still looking at their watches, the shoppers stacked up for the day, the mothers and *au pair* girls finishing tea, the pubs not yet open, the fathers not returned. Nobody was about. Possibly Cressida had gone to Ellis, but she didn't think so. She thought, rightly, that the girl was walking somewhere, walking fast in no particular direction. She went back into the kitchen. Now she wanted to telephone Graham, to ask him for help and advice. She could hear it without telephoning him: the girl's perfectly right, it's none of your business. She looked out of the window. They were all lying on the lawn, Daphne, Hereward, Jessica, Juniper.

'What's wrong with this lawn,' she heard Jessica say, 'is that there aren't any daisies.'

16

'It seems my sister Daphne is marrying someone called Here-ward. Do you believe it?'

'No,' Marcel said.

'Well, it must be true, Madam's written it—H-e-r-e-w-a-r-d. Do you think his surname can possibly be Wake?'

'I don't know,' Marcel yawned. He was not well acquainted with English history.

'I suppose one will have to go. To the wedding, I mean.'

'As you wish.' Marcel preferred them to speak English together because he thought his English was superior to Marcus's French. When they were having one of their frequent enjoyable quarrels they spoke both languages at once. This led to many misunderstandings.

'What shall I wear?'

'Oh, nobody shall care what you wear. It's your sister who is marrying, not you. And whatever you wear you will look like a peahen.'

'Thanks very much,' Marcus said. 'I think you mean peacock.'

Marcel was reading the paper. 'Beckett has written a play lasting for fifteen seconds.'

'I knew a man at Cambridge whose name was "huh". Just an apostrophe. Naturally he was Chinese.'

'Why bother to write one at all?'

'That,' Marcus said, 'is exactly why I don't.'

'When will you go to this wedding?'

'It's on August 2nd. I might go a day or two earlier, perhaps I can give Madam a hand. It's quite a production, a wedding.'

'She will get on better without you,' Marcel said. 'Fluttering.'

'I do not flutter.'

'You will make a mess of everything.'

'You mean *you* don't know how *you'll* get on without me. Nothing but tinned canneloni.'

'There you are perfectly wrong. I get along without you very well.'

'Of course I do . . .' Marcus sang, quavering, 'though not perhaps in spring . . .'

'Oh, go to your wedding.' Marcel threw down the newspaper and buttoned the frog fastenings on his velvet jacket. 'When will you be back?'

'On August 3rd. Unless'—his remarkable face twitched into a kind of shadow—'unless Madam needs me.'

'Who needs you?'

'Well. You do.'

'*C'est vrai*,' Marcel said, capitulating for once. They kissed perfunctorily and Marcel went off to the theatre. Marcus, after clearing away the breakfast things, sat down to Kafka, but his heart wasn't in it and he dreamed, lazily massaging the poodle's head with one hand. Imagine little Daphne getting married. Pretty little thing. Little thing? She was enormous. He must buy her a beautiful wedding present. That could take up a whole day, by the time one had been to the market and prepared the evening meal and made a few telephone calls. And something to wear. Not white, that would be bad taste. Perhaps pale, very pale lemon, with something mad like a tangerine scarf. Dear bloody Mother, with married daughters. Dear bloody Mother. If Daphne had a child, grandmother. My mother is a grandmother: it sounded odd.

And what about that bastard, that Claudius, that schmok who purported to be a father? He'd be there, of course. Taking all the credit, sitting on his fat arse in the middle of it all like a king. Christ, I shan't go. Christ, I will *not* be party to anything that has anything to do with him.

He dug his fingers into his blonde hair, then shook his head like a dog. Bad thinking. It's Madam's do. And Daphne's, of course. When he visited London he always stayed with friends, or in an hotel. He must find out whether there was room for him in that vast mansion of hers. It would be good, very good, to stay with her again. Of course, there was that little pipsqueak Philip, whom he hadn't seen for over a year. Presumably he'd be there in his grubby jeans with his great man's hands and his swaggering walk which seemed to say I'm real tough, man, I'm not a fuckin' queen like brother Marcus . . .

He wasn't getting anywhere. He was merely agitating himself. He dialled Eleanor's number. A low, hesitant voice answered : 'Hullo?'

'Hullo? Who's that?'

'What do you want?'

'Mrs. Strathearn.'

'Is that you, Marcus? This is Cressida.'

'Cressie. Well.' All thought deserted him. 'How are you?'

'Fine. Are you coming to the wedding?'

'Of course.'

'Good. Will you look very pretty?' she asked.

'I hope so.'

'It's not fair if you look too pretty. People are meant to notice Daphne, you know. Not you.'

It was, thank God, the same banter they had carried on for years. Nothing was changed. He said, 'I'm longing to see you.'

'I wear dresses all the time now. It's my new thing.'

'A great improvement. Do you also clean your fingernails?'

'Sometimes. Hang on. I'll get Mum.'

There was a long silence. Maybe she was in the bath or something. Then, breathless: 'Hullo? Marcus? I'm sorry, darling, I was at the top of the house . . .'

'Is it a very long house?'

'Very.'

'But don't you have telephones on every floor?'

'Yes, but you see . . . oh, never mind.' He could imagine her exactly, pushing back her hair in the same way that he did; reaching, probably, for a cigarette. 'Did you get my letter?' Yes, he heard the click of a lighter, the exhaling of breath.

'Yes. And of course I'll come. Can I stay with you?'

There was a moment's hesitation. 'Darling, the house is absurdly small. There are only three bedrooms, and there's me and Cressida and Philip. If you don't mind doubling up with Philip. Or sleeping on a sofa? It's a very comfortable sofa.'

He couldn't imagine anything he would like less. Nevertheless, to his astonishment, he heard himself saying, 'A sofa would be fine. I don't think doubling up with Philip is a very good idea.'

He could hear her frowning. 'No. Perhaps not. Well, anyway, the sofa is yours.'

'I'll come about the thirty-first. In case I can help or anything.'

'All right.' Did she sound reluctant? 'Will you bring some Jolie Madame?'

'You mean you still use Jolie Madame?'

'Sometimes. Don't you like it?'

'I'll bring you something better . . .'

She laughed. The sound, to him, was a hot drink on a cold day, crumpets, blankets, a door closed from the inside, a light turned on: 'All right. I'll see you on Thursday week.'

'All right. Bless you.'

When he put the phone down he thought of a thousand things—at least six—that he had wanted to ask her. Never mind. He would leave Kafka halfway through his tormented teens, and go shopping. He put the poodle on a lead, slung an Ibizan basket over his shoulder, and stepped out beautifully into the day.

．　　　．　　　．　　　．

'Oh God,' Philip said, 'my sister's getting married.'

'Bad luck,' his friend said. 'Mine did too. It was hell. They're not doing it in church, of course?'

'No. Hampstead Register Office.'

'The church thing is too much. It's not too bad in a register office. Even so, my mother cried the whole time. It was absolutely ghastly.'

'I don't see what they want to get married for,' Philip said, genuinely perplexed.

'What's his name?'

'I don't know.' It was a lie. Ever since Eleanor had told him, that weekend, he had tried to believe it wasn't true: Hereward.

'Do you like her? Your sister?'

'She's all right.'

'I don't like mine much, so I don't miss her or anything.'

'Mine doesn't live at home anyway.'

'Oh well then . . . it doesn't make much difference, does it?'

'Did you see that advert in the paper? About Afghanistan?' Philip asked.

'What advert?'

'Here. I've got it somewhere . . .'

' "Northern Afghanistan Expedition . . . young mixed group departs December for two and a half months to Kabul by Land Rover then heading north to the Oxus plain to visit the Turcoman tribes. Cost £169 return . . . Also expeditions to Everest"—gosh—"Western Nepal, India and the Sahara . . ." You're not actually thinking of going, are you?'

'Why not? Get away from all these plastic people.'

'Have you got £169?'

'No. But I could probably get it,' Philip mumbled.

'How?'

'I don't know. Somehow.'

'But it's for two and a half months. You'd miss school.'

'So? Don't you think I'd learn more from the Turcoman tribes than I would in this fucking place?'

'I think you're a bit mad. What about your mother?'

'My mother,' Philip said, his heart lurching, 'would have to lump it, wouldn't she?'

'Well . . .' his friend said. '*I* don't know.'

.   .   .   .   .

Cressida had apologised. Eleanor had apologised. Ellis, feeling he had created some disquiet, apologised. It made not the slightest difference to their feelings, which remained complex, loving and antagonistic. Eleanor began to tidy the landings and buy lampshades for the wedding. One afternoon, when she was just on her way out to the shops, Kilcannon rang.

She tried to sound distant. In fact, at the sound of his voice, her breath was mingling with his. 'Are you better?'

'Better?'

'You sent a wire to say you were . . . hospitalised.'

'Oh yes. I was. They put me to sleep for a couple of days. It does wonders for one's outlook on life. How are you?'

'I'm . . . all right.'

'I want to see you.'

'Well, then . . .' She breathed a small laugh. 'See me.'

'When are you free?'

'All the time.'

'Then what about . . . wait a minute, I'm looking in my book . . . I go back to Galway on the fourth, probably for a couple of months . . . Could you make lunch on the second?'

She couldn't say anything.

'Hullo? Are you there?'

'Yes. I'm sorry. My . . . my daughter's getting married on the second.'

'Your daughter? Married? I don't believe it. What is she, a child bride or something?'

'No.'

'Then you can't lunch on the second?'

'No.'

'Well, what else can we do . . . hell, it looks disastrous. I might be able to get out of something on the thirty-first . . . I'll have to ring you.'

'All right.'

'Life's hell, isn't it?'

'Sometimes.'

'You sound rather low.'

'Do I?'

'Well, I'm low, too. Believe me. I need to talk to you. Everything's quite . . . inextricably confused. You know what I mean?'

'Not really. You mean in general or . . . ?'

'Well, never mind. I don't want to bother you with my worries. I'll ring you when I can. All right?'

'All right.'

'And have a lovely wedding, though I still don't believe it.'

'Thank you. Goodbye.'

'Goodbye.'

A click, and he was gone. Why hadn't she said '*I* need to see *you*. Drop everything and come now, now this instant, now before I've even put the telephone down'? Why hadn't she said . . . ? She looked at her empty basket, a receptacle for something she had been going to buy. She looked at her handbag, her hands, her bare arms, her foot with the sandal swinging off the toes. Eleanor Strathearn. The cat who walked alone. How the elephant got its trunk, the leopard its spots. How Eleanor Strathearn grew old after her time. Marcus,

Cressida, Ellis, Daphne, Hereward, Jessica, Brian, Juniper. Graham. Philip. But I am utterly alone. I walk through the shops alone and drive alone in my car, I sleep alone and get up in the morning alone, and at night turn out the lights and go up the stairs alone. She was not even sad. It was as though someone were describing her to herself. Someone surrounded by hope and love, with no hope or love at all. Someone dead.

The telephone rang again. It was Daphne.

'Look, they're making a hell of a mess of this wedding list. We've already been bought two digital clocks and three giant-sized jasmine-scented candles. I mean, what does one *do*? Still, we had dinner with Dad last night and I must say it was a great success, he and Hereward got quite sloshed and that girl was positively shocked. Do you think she *thinks* anything? I mean, there was Dad talking away as though you were still married, I don't know what she can think, poor little thing, it's all very strange . . .'

She held the receiver about two inches away from her ear, and let the sound prattle on. It didn't matter. In a few moments there would be a slight whirring sound, and life would begin to move again. At the moment she was petrified, hard and still and cold as marble.

17

The whirring sound began: she moved, she spoke, she even laughed. A fine way for a bride's mother to go on. Something frightening was happening to her. A different type of woman would have asked for help, stammered some part of it out to some faceless psychiatrist whose only comment would be a gentle and encouraging 'Yes . . . ?' She was not that type of woman. Graham's faith in his drugs was unknown; as a doctor he may have been expert, though possibly too adventurous. As a man, he was deeply averse to prying into unnecessary depths: let sleeping neuroses lie, and with any luck they will slumber on for the rest of your life. For this reason he was extremely unpopular in the psychiatric world, and regarded by some as a dangerous quack. He hated this criticism, as he hated all criticism. Eleanor, not thinking, had taken his word for it. She had never tried his drugs, largely, perhaps, because he had never offered them to her. As far as Graham was concerned, Eleanor was sound as a bell, though possibly prone, like all women, to monthly bouts of hysteria. Whatever else she was, she was not his patient. Therefore when Daphne and Jessica told him that Eleanor was poorly, thin and tense and obviously given to secret weeping, he blotted it out of his mind as he blotted the tears from the cheeks of his rich and/or pretty patients. Eleanor was all right. Eleanor must be all right. It would be an insult to him if Eleanor was not all right.

The preparations for the wedding continued, largely commanded by Daphne. The writer, realising that he was on the losing side, had become unaccountably generous, giving her days off and a very complicated piece of do-it-yourself Japanese sculpture. The flat was re-painted and a large section of the sitting room rebuilt to house Hereward's stereo equipment. Daphne herself began to show signs of strain. Except for Jessica, they were, at this time, a gloomy lot. Daphne's dress was disaster, the sleeves too short, the bust too low, a wrinkle across the shoulders where no wrinkle should be. She wanted to scrap all seventy-five guineas' worth of it, but Eleanor went with her to the male dressmaker who called himself a couturier, and they sorted it out to Daphne's moderate satisfaction. Hereward remained unaccountably breezy, which, Daphne said, drove her mad. Hereward's family was contacted and turned out to be immense, at least four uncles and six aunts and four grandparents and an uncountable number of cousins, quite apart from his two sisters, who were both excessively pretty and lived on air, and the boy-friends they could not spend a minute without. As far as Daphne's relatives were concerned, there were only the two grandmothers, the two sisters and two brothers, and her separated parents. She had a few girl-friends and ex-lovers who might fill in the gaps, but there were obviously going to be gaps, the house would be like a beach in August. The caterers, two well-meaning girls whom Graham had got on the cheap, seemed to think that a few poorly lilies of the valley set about in small cut-glass vases constituted decoration. Eleanor ordered bucketfuls of flowers. Daphne told her to send the bill to Graham, but she didn't.

Marcus arrived, very nervous. At the sight of him standing in the doorway in the sun, the most beautiful and elegant and strange of all her children, Eleanor took him warmly in her arms. Philip, back from school, happening to witness this scene, went out for a long walk and was late for lunch.

'Darling, it's divine,' Marcus said. 'It's a perfect house.

Don't you absolutely love it?' He had brought innumerable presents, as many for Eleanor as for Daphne. The mantelpieces began to fill up with ornaments. There were great decanters of perfume, musky and bitter. 'For Daphne,' he said, 'I thought something a little lighter, a little more . . . bridal.' He tried out the sofa and found it absolute luxury.

Between the three of them, Marcus, Cressida and Philip, Eleanor found herself torn and distracted. From each of them she could have gained pleasure, to each of them she could have given pleasure, but the three of them, concentrated on her, with no father to take part of the attention, became too much. She actually found herself telephoning Graham and asking him if he would have Philip to supper. He said he was giving a dinner party. She said all right, let Philip be part of the dinner party. He said he might well have to leave it in the middle, if he was needed. She said that in that case he should send Philip home. The conversation was bitter, and at cross-purposes. Gwen had come home, and Cressida was moping. Eleanor rang Alex, in the hope of finding some sort of comfort.

'So glad you rang, darling. The contract was signed today. I'm a house owner.'

'Oh. Good.'

'We have apples and pears and mulberries and a vine. No furniture, though.'

She tried her best. 'Who needs furniture?'

'Well, we've got a bed. When we've got two, you must come and stay.'

'I'm going to Greece with Philip next week.'

'Ah, so you are. When you come back, then. And we'll see you at the wedding. How's it going? All right?'

'Oh, yes,' she said. 'Fine. How's Georgina?'

'She's got rather a nasty cold, actually. But she sends her love.'

'Thank you.'

Life is sometimes like this. It doesn't progress smoothly

from minute to minute, neatly accumulating into months and years. It jerks and jumps, great lumps of it are missing. What happened last Wednesday? Yesterday afternoon was a yawning hole in which there was no time at all; this morning, on the other hand, tripped neatly from nine to ten to eleven and then suddenly stopped, as though it had come up against some insuperable obstacle. Philip had gone back to school; now Philip was home again. What had happened in between? Today was perhaps Thursday. On Saturday Daphne was getting married. What would happen to Friday? Only one thing was certain in the mists in which she bumped up against objects which happened to be meals, or people, or necessary demands: Graham. He was working, he was living, he was giving dinner parties, he was making some kind of love to Nell Partwhistle. Graham was real. He showed no concern for her, or for any of the children except Philip. He did not want to meet Marcus. He did not care about Cressida. He thought Daphne's wedding an unnecessary and expensive bore. He gave money to Jessica which was, for him, a very genuine expression of love. He was on a diet, and this took a lot of his attention. Eleanor thought, after she had telephoned Alex, of ringing Graham at Wimpole Street and saying, quite matter-of-factly, 'I think I'm dying.' He would probably have said that he might be able to fit her in next Monday week at six. She knew that she wasn't being fair, but what was fair in such hateful peace?

On Friday morning she received a letter from an old, old lover whom she had not seen for ten years. He was French, his English bad and his handwriting illegible. The letter had been forwarded to numerous addresses and was dated the previous January. 'I take you in my arms,' it ended, 'and hold you tightly.' Perhaps, translated from the French, this was a polite phrase meaning no more than 'Yours sincerely'. Nevertheless she stuck it on the wall of her heart, to be looked at when all else failed. The words contained all she needed.

On Friday evening when Philip had, as he called it, 'been

got rid of', and Cressida had gone round to comfort Daphne, who had decided that she didn't want to get married at all, Marcus and Eleanor went out to dinner at the bistro. There were more young marrieds than usual and the place was almost lively. Marcus looked at the menu with suspicion and had a long discussion with the head waiter, a heterosexual Italian, on the possible ingredients of the cassoulet. He was not satisfied and chose trout. The head waiter was sullen, and made an unnecessary fuss of Eleanor.

'Dearest Mama,' Marcus said, 'I have come to a decision and I warn you no one, but no one, is going to talk me out of it. I am coming to Greece with you.'

'No,' she should have said, 'you're not.' Philip had made out an itinerary worthy of Hellenic Tours; he had measured distances and pored over guide-books and decided exactly where they were going and what they were going to see. He had made a list of hotels marked with stars and prices, and above all he had circled in red crayon his treasured, longed-for antiquities. Philip was taking her to Greece. 'But why?' she asked.

'The child says you're going north. You have no idea what the north can be like in August, appallingly hot and nowhere to stay, and neither of you speak a word of Greek . . .'

'We got on all right before,' she said rather tartly.

'You had Graham with you. At least he passes for a man. A woman and a child alone—it's madness, darling, pure madness. I can look after you and show you where to go . . .'

'But we know where we're going!'

'Meteora, he says. Now do you really want to see a lot of stupid monks sitting on top of a lot of dull rocks? I can show you beaches you wouldn't believe. And we can stay in fishermen's cottages and swim, and go dancing . . .'

'I don't think Philip much likes dancing.'

'Then he needn't. But I do promise you, it'll be hell if you go alone.' He took her hand across the table. 'Let me come. I'd like to look after you.'

160

One part of her was touched. The other part was fiercely loyal to Philip, her greatest love. 'I don't know . . .' she said. 'I'll have to talk to him about it.'

'The wretched child's only fifteen! Why not just tell him?'

'Because,' she said, 'that's not the way we do things. I do see what you mean.' In fact she already saw herself and Philip surrounded by bandits in the middle of the night on some mountain-top, and was not at all sure that Marcus might not be some comfort. 'But we must discuss it.'

'I can't see that there's anything to discuss,' he said, petulant. 'I'm coming.'

She could not say to him that of his own choice as much as anything else he was no longer really one of the family. She had a vague idea of his feelings for her, and they embarrassed her. Marcus's place was with Marcel in Paris, a distant, exquisite semi-son. In a way she wanted to be a mother to him, but did not feel so much motherly as moderately friendly and admiring. His need for her was too excessive, and too impossible to satisfy. Perhaps the necessary element of incest was lacking. She found him decorative and amusing, but in some way he had wronged her. None of this was clearly understood, and could certainly never be explained. She patted his hand. 'We'll see,' she said. 'It would be nice.'

It was only ten o'clock when they had finished dinner, and he suggested that they went to the pub—'Some really filthy, sordid English pub with beer spilt on the counters, you know.' So she took him to the local, the nearest and most sordid pub she knew. They went into the saloon bar. The girl in the PVC mackintosh—did she never wear anything else?—was sitting on a stool in the corner. Marcus ordered two brandies. He looked so astounding in this setting that everyone momentarily broke into silence, shuffling their beer mugs and nudging each other surreptitiously.

'What a happy place,' he said, looking round. 'How I wish Marcel were here. One forgets how *gay* the English are.'

'Well, you wanted to come.'

'I did indeed.' He was looking at the girl in the PVC. 'And all sorts, too. Dykey ladies.'

'Don't be silly. She's a perfectly ordinary girl.'

'Have you seen her before?'

'A few times. She's always coming in here.' For some reason she had turned her back on the girl. 'Why do you think she's . . . ?'

'Wait and see.'

An older woman came in, dressed in jeans and a shirt; she was too fat for either, but merry-looking. She took the stool next to the girl's and they started to talk in a desultory way of people who know each other too well, and are perhaps rather bored.

'Not a success,' Marcus said. '*That* won't last long.'

She was half displeased, half interested. 'You think everyone's like you,' she said.

'So they are, most of them. They just don't admit it.'

'I don't believe you.'

'I bet I'm happier with Marcel than you ever were with our father, who unfortunately isn't in heaven. I mean, heterosexual men are such bores.'

'And heterosexual women?'

'I'm sorry for them. They have to try and pretend to be mad about the bores.'

'But supposing they're not pretending? I mean, sexually . . . men and women . . . fit.'

He looked at her under his blond hair, his eyes slightly slanted like her own, his mouth composed in gentle scorn. 'Is that your experience . . . at the moment?'

She drained her brandy and laughed. 'I don't have any experience. At the moment.'

'What about this knight Jessica told me about?'

'He doesn't exist.'

'You mean really doesn't exist?'

'I suppose he does somewhere. On the telephone occasionally.'

'You fancied him?'

'Oh, Marcus . . .' She mocked him, conscious that the woman and the girl were talking about him. 'Yes, I fancied him.'

'And you think you and he would have . . . fitted?'

'Oh, I don't know! At least the . . . mechanism . . . is right.'

'Darling Mother, what you want isn't mechanism. It's love.'

'It would be nice to have both.'

'It would be nice to be the Aga Khan. Particularly a queer Aga Khan.'

'You and Marcel have both.'

'Not what is known as "normally". Though I agree it's a lot easier for men.'

'I don't see it,' she said, puzzling. 'I don't see it.'

'Look: heteros of your age go for dolly birds. Right? Unless you have a faithful and devoted husband, which you don't, where do you find this love?'

'I don't know.'

'You just keep hoping, don't you? Making up fairy stories about knights?'

'Not fairy stories,' she said, and giggled wretchedly.

'Oh, you poor old thing.' He put his arm around her and ordered more brandies. 'You poor beautiful thing. It's not fair, is it?'

'If you keep on like that,' she said, 'I shall cry.'

'All right. I'll stop. Shall we talk to the dykes?'

'No.'

'Shall we talk about Daphne and her lovely wedding? Shall I like Hereward?'

'I should think so. He's very good-looking.'

'More good-looking than me?'

'Different.'

'Anyway, I only like older men. They may be a bit fat, but they're solid. Do you know I've only twice been unfaithful to Marcel?'

'I don't want to hear.'

'Do you find it a great strain, having a queer son?'

'I don't often think about it.'

'But you're happier with that manly great Philip?'

'Is he manly?' she asked, with pleasure.

'Oh, straight as a die.'

'I'm happy with all of you,' she said. 'In one way or another.'

'I wish to God I could help you,' he said.

It was raining slightly as they walked home. Philip had gone to bed, but still had his light on. She saw to her dismay and anguish that he had been crying, but he turned his head on the pillow and wouldn't let her look.

'How was the dinner party?' she asked awkwardly.

'A lot of plastic people. How was yours?'

'All right.' This was not the moment to tell him that Marcus wanted to come to Greece. 'It's merry wedding day tomorrow.'

He grunted.

She kissed lightly some tuft of hair that she could see.

'Love you.'

She turned out the light. As she went out of the room he said, 'Good night. So do I.'

18

In the waiting room at the register office Mrs. Bennet, in brown straw and beige linen, and Mrs. Strathearn, in pale pink, were introduced to Hereward's four grandparents, who were called Stagg and Phillips. At no point during the afternoon was anyone able to tell the difference between the Phillips and the Staggs, except that one of the grandfathers was deaf and one of the grandmothers was wearing a bright red beret. Hereward's parents, who were called Stagg, were easier to recognise, a casual couple coloured like the pine they stripped. Left wing, agnostic, and not much given to this kind of thing. Eleanor liked them immediately, particularly when they seemed to take it as a matter of course that Graham, owing to pressing business, was unable to be present. The rest of the family would appear at the reception. The two grandfathers, the four grandmothers, the two mothers and one father, and the two brothers and sisters, sat about as though waiting to have their teeth drawn. Eleanor and Mrs. Stagg junior smoked. Philip surreptitiously chewed gum. Marcus, as he had promised himself, was dressed in pale lemon with a tangerine scarf. His face dropped at the sight of Hereward and Daphne when they entered the waiting room.

They were both in white and looked almost absurdly beautiful. Daphne, from nerves and some instinctive grief over her long-lost virginity, drooped a little in the most becoming way. Neither of them smiled. Perhaps it really was the most serious moment of their lives. Eleanor found herself utterly amazed that she had helped to produce this exquisite, mournful beauty. Mrs. Stagg's face turned from stripped pine to the pale pink of intense emotion. Only Graham was not there. He was discussing cycloid symptoms with a young baroness who thought she was a manic depressive. As the baroness was free all day and all night every week of the year, this was not strictly necessary. Graham was a coward, and there were times when he clung to his cowardice like a lifebelt.

Hereward and Daphne went into the wedding room, followed by the relatives. A nice, clean, paternal-looking man was sitting behind a desk. He rose to welcome the couple, who then sat down with their backs to their families. Eleanor sat next to Mrs. Stagg. She wanted to attend, but her thoughts scattered hopelessly, flew to the ends of time. Her grief at Graham's absence, her memories of Graham's love for Daphne, her own memories of Daphne, the most absurd irrelevancies—such as the time when Daphne had bought a fur hat of which Graham had disapproved—flew round her brain and blocked her ears to the strictly non-religious homily which the paternal-looking man was giving them. Hereward's 'I will' was strong and clear, Daphne's most inaudible. It was time for the mothers to cry. Eleanor lent Mrs. Stagg, who did not look the crying kind, her handkerchief. She also passed a tissue to Daphne, who was overcome. It was, as Cressida said afterwards, more like a bloody wake than a wedding. At last the paternal-looking man wished them the best of luck, they kissed rather awkwardly, everyone blew their noses, and it was over.

The day was English summer at its best, blue and puffed white and gold and smothered with flowers. The catering girls were fussed, but at least the champagne was ready. Everyone went out into the garden, churning up the new grass with their heels. Uncles and aunts and cousins arrived, outnumbering the Strathearn family by four to one. Daphne looked more and more dazed, clinging to Hereward's arm as though she had lost the use of her lovely though invisible legs. Eleanor began to feel insanely like the Queen at a royal garden party. She shook what seemed like hundreds of anonymous hands and told scores of hopefully beaming faces that yes, she was the bride's mother.

'Dad's arrived,' Cressida said, as though it were a kind of secret password.

'Where?'

'I don't know. I saw him in the kitchen talking to the girls.'

Eleanor began to look for him. She saw Alex and Georgina, Ellis and Gwen. She went across the patio into Philip's room and found him lying on Philip's bed holding a glass of champagne.

'I'm tired,' he said amiably. 'How's it all going?'

'Couldn't you come out? Couldn't you talk to someone? Couldn't you just *try*?'

'They seem to be getting on very well without me.'

'She's your daughter! It's your bloody daughter who's getting married!'

'Oh, for heaven's sake . . .' He heaved his legs off the bed. 'What d'you want me to do, then?'

'Just care for once, that's all! Just *care*!'

She went and locked herself into Philip's shower room, and recovered, and used Cressida's make up and returned to the garden. Graham was talking to one of Hereward's ornamental sisters. Without a trace of apology she took his arm and led him to Mr. Stagg, who was peacefully smoking a pipe and reading the labels on the roses.

'This is Daphne's father,' she said. 'This is Hereward's father.'

Cressida was trying to avoid Ellis, who was trying to find her. Gwen, wan and quiet, was talking to Marcus. People were sitting on the steps leading down to the garden, and champagne glasses were balanced on the walls. A lot of pretty girls and boys had arrived, presumably friends of Hereward's.

Looking up the garden, she saw Jessica and Philip sitting on the grass with their backs against the wall. Jessica was wearing a Renaissance dress she had made out of a plum velvet curtain; Philip had a tight flowered shirt with a high collar and his long hair was clean and brushed.

'It's incredible,' Georgina was saying, 'how beautiful they all are.'

'Not when you look at their mother,' Alex said, and kissed Eleanor.

Mrs. Bennet had found a chair from somewhere and was sitting like the queen she was, the founder of a dynasty. Her brown straw hat was knocked a little to one side and she was having a vivacious conversation with one of the uncles. Mrs. Strathearn had stolen Marcus away from Gwen, and he was making her titter outrageously.

'How are you, Mum?' Daphne asked.

'All right,' Eleanor lied. 'How are you?'

'Bloody 'ell,' Daphne said, and turned graciously to greet a new relative.

Daphne, Hereward, and some of the chosen friends, were going back to the flat to put their feet up and, as Hereward said, get stoned out of their minds. The Staggs and the Phillips appeared to have plans which had something to do with the Café Royal. Mrs. Bennet was firmly going home on the six-fifteen from Paddington and Mrs. Strathearn's car had been waiting since half past five. By eight the garden began to empty. It looked as though it had been trampled by a herd of bulls. Somebody—no one seemed to know who—had suggested that Graham took Eleanor, Marcus, Cressida, Jessica and Philip out to dinner. Accordingly, in two cars and with grim inner faces, they went.

Graham obviously wanted to get the whole thing over as quickly as possible. He stated that no one wanted anything to begin with. Marcus said that, on the contrary, he wanted whitebait. Philip demanded tomato soup, in spite of his disgust that it was home-made. The women agreed to have nothing. It was Saturday evening, the restaurant full, the service slow. From long experience, Eleanor knew that Graham was going to lose his temper. Marcus, flanked by his father and his brother, was at his most camp, flaunting himself in every direction. Cressida had finally been caught by Ellis at the party; with three-quarters of a bottle of champagne in one hand, he had sworn his undying devotion to her and told her it was all over with Gwen. Far from making her exuberant, this had distressed her immensely. Jessica could find nothing on the menu to eat but salad. She was longing to get back to Brian and Juniper.

'Well!' Marcus said. 'We are a happy little family, aren't we?'

'Oh, shut up,' Philip growled.

'I wonder if there's any danger of our getting some food?' Graham snarled to a startled waiter.

'He's doing his best,' Jessica said.

Eleanor said nothing. Or, rather, she was not conscious of saying anything. Possibly she interposed a few comments here and there, made a few soothing noises. What she was saying to herself was It's no good, it's no good, it's no good. She looked almost furtively at Graham's furious face, his untidy suit; she felt his resentment as though it were unendurable heat or cold. He hates us. He may love us individually, in so far as he understands love. But he hates us. He resents every mouthful of food we eat. We are his enemies. Can it simply be because we make him feel so old? Can it simply be because they are all so beautiful and, mostly, kind, and, mostly, generous? Can it be jealousy? Why had he been Daphne's enemy, on her wedding day? Why, Graham, why?

'I ordered a bottle of wine at least twenty minutes ago!' He was almost screaming now. 'What the hell's the matter with this place tonight?'

'I think I'll go home,' Jessica said, and gathered up her velvet robe.

'Oh, don't go . . .' Eleanor pleaded.

'I've had my salad, anyway.'

'But how will you . . . ?'

'I'll get a bus. Good night, everyone.' She kissed Philip and Eleanor and left.

'You can get rid of all of us,' Marcus said to Graham, 'if you keep trying.'

For a terrible, and yet almost glorious, moment, Eleanor thought that Graham was going to get up and leave too. Something, perhaps the thought of Philip, kept him. For a few moments he was very quiet, and then he began to talk to Philip, who answered him cordially. The wine and the food arrived. Marcus became more subdued. There had been a victory and a defeat, but it was impossible to tell on whose side. Marcus asked Cressida about America. Eleanor, with Jessica's empty chair beside her, watched and waited. I take you in my arms and hold you tightly. What would that be in French? She must ask Marcus. She must tell Philip that Marcus wanted to come to Greece. She was drinking coffee, so the meal must be nearly over. Yes, they didn't even have to wait too long for the bill.

'So you'll get all the instructions, and the ticket, and the money and everything from Trixie on Monday,' Graham was saying. 'And I'll see you in Portugal.'

'Smashing,' Philip said.

'And have a good time in Greece. Both of you.'

'We will.'

'I've sent you a cheque, by the way,' he said, offhand, to Eleanor.

'Oh. Thank you.'

'Well, then . . .' He pushed back his chair. 'I must be off.'

They all got up, filed out into the warm summer night. On the pavement they stood about for a moment, all realising, in their different ways, that a parting was taking place.

'Where's your car?' Graham asked.

'Just behind yours.'

'Well, then. End of wedding day, thank God.'

'It was a pity you weren't there,' Eleanor said. 'I mean when they got married.'

'Sorry I couldn't make it too. Good night.' He kissed Philip, Cressida and Eleanor. 'Good night, Marcus.'

But Marcus had already walked away and got into Eleanor's car. Graham shot away into the darkness. Cressida got in next to Marcus in the back. Philip sat in the front. For a few seconds, before Eleanor switched on the engine, there was silence. They were gathering themselves together, each remembering again who they were. Then they went home.

19

'He's not coming!' Philip screamed. 'He's not coming! He's not! It was my idea! We were going together! What does he want to come for? Why does he want to butt in and spoil it all?'

His tears, the tears of a young man, were terrible. He was sitting, rocking with grief, in his armchair. Eleanor knelt on the floor in front of him and tried to hold him still, to hold him to her.

'But, Philip . . .'

'What does he mean we can't manage? I've worked it all out! I *know* what we're going to do! My God, anyone would think I couldn't look after you! What good would *he* be?'

'Then he won't come, darling, we won't take him.'

'But you want him to come! Obviously you do, or you'd never have suggested it! If he doesn't come now, it'll be all wrong, you won't like it, you never did just want to be with me, anyway!'

'Be quiet,' she said severely. 'Stop it. You know perfectly well I want to be with you.'

'Then why did you . . . ?'

'It's just that Marcus knows Greece, and he can speak Greek, and he doesn't see us very much, and he suggested that he might be helpful. That's all. If you feel so strongly about it, of course he won't come.'

He sobbed uncontrollably for a few minutes, while she still tried to hold him. Then, sniffing hard, he said, 'But he wouldn't want to do what we want to do.'

'Then he'd have to, wouldn't he?' She didn't tell him that Marcus had said that Philip's careful itinerary was pure madness.

'I know you don't see him much. I do know that.'

'It doesn't matter. I can always go over to Paris if I want to. It's just that I'm so . . . bloody lazy!'

He got up and found a grubby handkerchief and blew his nose hard.

'It's just . . . I wish he wasn't such an awful queer.'

'Is it? I mean, isn't it just that you don't want anyone else to come? Whether they're queer or not?'

'I don't know.' The storm was subsiding. He allowed her to hold his hand. 'I wouldn't have to share a room with him or anything?'

'Of course you wouldn't. Anyway, he's not coming.'

'Does he want to come very much?'

'Why don't you ask him?'

'I don't know.'

'Look . . .' She felt, and sounded, conspiratorial. '*If* he came, and we didn't . . . well, it didn't work . . . we could always get rid of him.'

'How?' He almost grinned, slimy with tears.

'Just tell him to bugger off.'

'Marcus?'

'Why not? It's our trip. It's our holiday. I mean, *we* didn't ask him, did we?'

'Do you want him to come? Really?'

'I don't know,' she said honestly. 'I feel sort of . . . guilty about him, I suppose. And he really thinks he can help us. He might be able to show us a lot of things we don't know about. I'd honestly sooner go with you, but . . .'

'Let's talk about it later,' he said.

'All right.'

She was cooking the lunch when he came in with his face washed and his hands safe in his pockets. He wandered about a bit, nibbling cheese and inspecting the kitchen as though he had not really noticed it before. Then he said, 'Okay. He can come if he wants to.'

She was both relieved and disappointed. 'You're sure?'

'I don't suppose it'll make much difference.'

Owing largely to Philip's efficiency, they had their tickets to Athens, their hotel booked, and a hired car waiting for them. Now they also had Graham's cheque which—although he had not actually made it out to Philip—seemed to Eleanor exorbitant. Marcus, it appeared, did not have the money for his fare. Eleanor knew nothing about his finances, but imagined, from the lavish presents and the way he lived, that he was fairly well off. He said he would wire Paris for some money to be sent to Athens, but in the meanwhile could she lend him enough for his fare. She did so, willingly.

.   .   .   .   .

On the evening before they left, Graham came for a drink. He and Nell Partwhistle were leaving for Portugal in a few days and he was in a mellow mood. Marcus had gone out to see friends, Philip and Cressida drifted away after a little small talk, almost as though they were tactfully leaving a couple of lovers. They sat in the garden drinking cold white wine. Graham, because of his diet, mixed his with soda water.

'I'm sorry about the other evening. I know I behaved appallingly.'

'It's all right. Everyone was a bit . . . strained.'

'The last thing I want to do is to make you unhappy.'

In the summer evening and the intimacy of parting she allowed herself to believe it as much as he did. 'It doesn't matter.' And she made herself say, 'You'll have a good holiday in Portugal.'

'I'm tired out.'

He looked it. 'Yes. I know. Doesn't . . . Partwhistle look after you at all?'

'Not really. It's probably because I won't let her.'

'Does she do anything?'

'I suppose she'll have to go.' It was as though he were talking about some pet that would sooner or later have to be destroyed.

'Oh, well . . .' She wouldn't allow herself a moment of triumph, or hope. She knew he was not telling the truth, but the lies were too comforting to spoil.

He talked about his work. The shadows lengthened to cover the whole garden, but it was still warm. Somewhere up in the house Philip was playing his guitar. Graham was completely sober, but exhaustion, or the peace of the evening, made him talk with a kind of insane gentleness.

'We'll get married in October.'

'Who will?'

'You and me. I'm sure we'll be together in the autumn.'

She smiled. 'Where?'

'I think I'll come and live here. Would that be all right?'

'If you want to,' she said casually.

'You know I love you.'

'I love you too.'

It was a complete fantasy. He would never remember saying these things. She would remember them always, with grief and bitterness and a dreadful sense of betrayal. He was making himself happy. She was helping him to be happy. It was getting dark. He didn't want to go. They sat a few feet apart, stretched out in their chairs, drinking a second bottle of wine. For the first time in her life, it seemed, she was not lonely.

'Well . . .' he said. 'I suppose I must go and cook the supper.'

'It's ridiculous,' she said indignantly. 'Can't she even cook?'

He grinned. 'Oh, she does the rough.' Even that wasn't true, but he liked the sound of it.

'What happens when you have to go out, to see people?'
He shrugged. 'No supper.'

He was standing up. He was going. He kissed her on the mouth and she held him tightly, the familiar, inaccessible bulk that no longer belonged to her. She was not sad. In fact she was light-hearted, drunk with the fantasy of the last two hours. They wished each other happy holidays and said they would meet again in September. She did not go into the house with him but stayed for a little while in the garden, trying to preserve the spell.

20

The first surprise in Athens was a large square Greek who met them at the airport, kissed Marcus on both cheeks and insisted on carrying all their luggage.

'Theo,' Marcus said briefly. 'An old friend.'

'Eleftherios,' the friend said. 'But Theo is more easy. At which hotel do you stay?'

Eleanor told him the Grande Bretagne. He looked at Marcus with bewilderment. Marcus shrugged his shoulders as though in shame.

'We'll go there first,' he said. 'I'll stay with you if that's all right.'

'That is what I was expecting,' said Theo.

In the taxi Marcus and the friend talked in Greek.

'We're wondering where we shall take you to dinner tonight,' Marcus said. 'There's a divine little taverna . . .'

'We're going to Turkeliminos,' Philip said. 'We like it there.'

'But, my dear child, why? The food's appalling and it's crammed with tourists.'

'We're tourists,' Philip said.

'Mother, for heaven's sake persuade the boy to be a little more adventurous. Besides, it's horribly pricey.'

Start, Eleanor told herself firmly, as you intend to go on.

'We do rather like it there,' she said. 'But you and . . . Theo don't have to come.'

'My dear, I wouldn't dream of it!' The beautiful face had become sullen as a rock. He turned his attention to Theo. They seemed to have a lot to talk about, and she wondered whether Theo was one of Marcus's two infidelities. Philip looked out of the window and pursed his lips as though he were whistling, though no sound came out.

They decided to meet for a drink in Sintagma Square at six. Eleanor and Philip had adjoining rooms and talked as they washed and changed, but not about Marcus and Theo. they did not mention plans of any kind. Both were making up their minds, but both were determined to be private about it.

Sintagma Square was hot, stifling, as though it were under canvas. Marcus and Theo were already there, drinking neat ouzo. Philip also ordered ouzo. Eleanor noticed for the first time that his jaw muscles were clenching and unclenching, a curiously adult symptom of tension.

'Now, darlings,' Marcus said, 'about your plans. I've been talking to Theo and he agrees that it's pure madness to drive up to Kavala. We must put the car on a boat at Piraeus, it's the only possible way. Then we can go over to Thassos and find some gorgeous beach, and lie about. I mean you don't *really* want to see those dreary old ruins, do you?'

'Yes,' Eleanor said quickly. 'We do.'

'I would never have believed,' said Theo, with a certain gentle charm, 'that the mother of Marcus would be a sightseer.'

'If there are sights to see,' Philip said, 'what's wrong with seeing them?'

'It's just so . . . vulgar,' Marcus said.

'Okay. We're vulgar.'

'About this boat . . .' Eleanor said. 'We can go all the way to Kavala?'

'Of course.'

She appealed to Philip. 'Wouldn't it be rather nice? Then we could drive back and see Meteora and Joannina and Dodona and everything. We could stop in Delphi.'

'Delphi!' Marcus sighed, giving up hope.

'Maybe it wouldn't be too bad,' Philip said grudgingly.

'How long does it take?'

'Oh, eight, nine hours. And extremely comfortable. I will go now to the travel agent and fix it. You have a Fiat car? And you wish first or second class?'

'First,' Philip said.

'And cabins also?'

'Also cabins.'

'I can't afford it,' Marcus said. 'Sorry.'

'Yes, you can,' Eleanor said, although she was worried. Did he have *any* money, or was he really just being taken on a holiday by Mother? 'I'll pay.'

'Well, I won't have a cabin, then. They're vilely stuffy, anyway. Will you fix that, Theo?'

'Of course.' Smiling, Theo waited with his hand held out, which Eleanor stuffed with drachmas.

'Will that be enough?' she asked anxiously.

'If not, I will tell you. I myself will travel third class.'

He walked away across the square. There was a dreadful silence.

'You mean,' Eleanor asked with difficulty, 'that Theo is coming too?'

'Why? Don't you like him?'

'Of course, but . . .'

'He's my friend,' Marcus said with dignity.

'If he comes,' Philip said rather simply, as though making an unimportant comment, 'I'm going home.'

'You are a filthy little snob,' Marcus said.

'Yes,' Philip said, 'I probably am. And I don't like queers.'

'Oh, shut up!' Eleanor snapped. They both looked at her, alarmed. She waited a few moments, then took command. 'The boat idea seems sensible. We thought'—to Marcus—'it would be nice if you came with us. But we didn't cater for your friends, however charming they may be. I don't think it's a good idea if Theo comes with us. And I don't intend to pay for him. Even third class. If you would rather stay in Athens with him, that's fine. Now Philip and I are going out to dinner. If you would ask Theo to be kind enough to leave the tickets and the change, if there is any, with the hall porter. We shan't be late. Ring my room about eleven and tell me what you've decided. I hope you come.'

She stood up and Philip, her page, stood beside her.

'I'm sorry,' Marcus said.

'I'm sorry too,' Philip said.

For some extraordinary reason, which neither of them could ever puzzle out, the two brothers shook hands.

.　　　.　　　.　　　.

Finding the boat at Piraeus was, finally, ludicrous. Parked in the blazing sun, jammed between huge screaming lorries while Marcus hurried from office to office, his face puckered with anxiety, Eleanor found herself helplessly laughing, bowed over the steering wheel of the car as though in some kind of jovial pain.

'What's the matter?' Philip asked anxiously.

'I don't know!'

'Do you think he can actually . . . speak Greek?'

'I don't know!'

'Well, I don't see what's so funny.'

'Neither do I,' she said. 'Except that we haven't got Theo.'

He snorted happily. 'No,' he said. 'We haven't got Theo.'

At last the boat was located. Compared with its gleaming white neighbours it looked like a tramp steamer. The car had to be hauled on deck by ropes and then driven by Eleanor—Marcus said he couldn't face it—into some floating dungeon where Greek sailors screamed obscenities which could not possibly mean 'left hand down, right hand down'. Her rather hysterical gaiety went through blazing rage into feminine despair. 'Then *you* do it,' she said to an enormous sailor who appeared to be threatening her. She got out of the car and he lifted it bodily and put it in its right place. She found her way to the cabins, where Philip was making himself comfortable. When they found the first-class bar it was like a *fin de siècle* drawing room, with little plush curtains and gilt ornaments and fussy mirrors.

'I think I'm going to like this,' Philip said. 'Can I have an ouzo?'

'You drink too much.'

'Only ouzo.'

She went and lay on a comfortable chair on deck, looking myopically out to sea. Marcus had disappeared. She felt peaceful. Thousands of miles away, Graham was injecting some valuable bottom, or peering into the dark recesses of some aristocratic throat. Graham was thousands of miles away. And Cressida, alone in the house? Most probably sleeping. But she, Eleanor, was limp, relaxed, secure. And what about the torturers, the political prisoners, the martyrs so much nearer, so much more important than Graham and Cressida? 'Greece . . .' she said to herself, and the word slithered through her body, gave her a history, gave her a past.

'What are you thinking about?' Marcus asked, lowering himself on to a chair beside her.

'That I have no political conscience. Or else I wouldn't be here.'

'I've been down in the third class. They're all there.'

'They can't help it.'

'They enjoy it. They're dancing already.'

'While Rome burns.'

'Oh, nonsense. Really, Mother darling, that sort of thing is just a bore.'

'The thing is, we never got much civilisation from Germany, really. Except Bach. And Goethe. And Schiller. And they were much too late in the day.'

'I've no idea what you're talking about.'

'Yes, you have. You *have*, Marcus. You're not stupid.'

'Sometimes I prefer to be.'

'Oh well, then . . .'

The engines started. The boat tore itself away from the dock with the most enormous grinding and tearing and shouting. Suddenly, like a slide slotted into her brain, Eleanor saw a picture of her house, her home: its tall windows, panelled front door, the smaller windows at the top which were those of her white, her whitish, bedrooms, the steps up to the front door, the unpolished brass knocker. She had left home. She was homeless. Just now, with the sea stretching far, and the mainland falling back, the thought was oddly comforting.

.   .   .   .   .

'What time do we get to Kavala?' Eleanor asked the waiter at dinner.

'Kavala? About . . .' His hands circled a clock a number of times. 'Two o'clock maybe.'

'In the morning, you mean? In the night?'

'In the night? No. In the day. The afternoon.'

'*Tomorrow* afternoon?'

'That's right.'

Marcus streamed off into torrential Greek. The waiter was puzzled.

'We get to Kavala,' he said, 'at two o'clock in the day. tomorrow. About.'

'But we were told it took eight or nine hours!'

'Whoever told you,' the waiter said, 'was a big joker.'

Both Eleanor and Philip looked, unfairly, at Marcus.

'It's not my fault,' he said.

'No,' Eleanor said, 'of course it isn't.'

'It's Theo's,' Philip said, and crammed his mouth with spaghetti.

Marcus got up and began to talk to the waiter in Greek.

The waiter insisted on replying in English. Eleanor began to laugh again.

'What *is* the matter?' Philip asked, feeling out of it.

'Well . . . I mean . . . it doesn't matter! And I don't think the waiter *understands* Greek!'

'Perhaps he just doesn't understand Marcus,' Philip said.

'Do try,' Eleanor said, without much conviction.

'I am trying.'

Marcus came back. 'Well,' he said, 'there seems to have been a mistake. We get in at two o'clock tomorrow afternoon.'

'Yes,' Philip said. 'We know.'

'I think I'll go down to the third class and see what's going on. D'you want to come?'

'No, thank you,' Philip said.

When Marcus had gone, Eleanor, rather disappointed, said, 'It might have been fun. He says they're dancing.'

'It's like looking at animals in the zoo,' Philip said. 'They don't want us watching them. I should feel a fool.'

'They wouldn't mind.'

'No . . . but I would.'

'You're a bit priggish sometimes, you know.'

He flushed, unbearably vulnerable to criticism. 'You go, then, if you want to. I'm going to read my book.'

He went away and she ordered another half-bottle of domestica and sat alone in the empty dining room. She had a fantasy, which was often to recur, that she was not here with her two awkward sons, but with Kilcannon. They were chugging gently up the Aegean and he was holding her hand across the stained tablecloth and soon they would go up and sit on deck and wait for the islands to grow out of the sea, and not talk very much, because there would be no problems, no sadness, no loneliness.

'The bill?' the waiter asked.

'Of course,' she said, and paid it.

.   .   .   .   .

183

It was about eleven o'clock the next morning when they discovered that the car had been disembarked in the middle of the night and dumped on Limnos. Why, nobody knew. How, nobody knew. Marcus spoke very rapidly, and with remarkable control, to various officers in neat uniforms who shrugged their shoulders and smiled. They read the car's ticket with interest, and pointed out to each other that it was made out for Kavala. Amazing, they said. Philip went and lay on a bench and read *Catch 22*, disassociating himself from the whole thing. He did not even say I told you so. Through the drama of the car, Marcus struck up a friendship with one of the junior officers and they sat in the bar drinking retsina and talking very earnestly. Eleanor began to feel that she was travelling alone. She sat in the sun and read a novel with her eyes, while her thoughts drifted and her heart ached and her legs browned.

They would have to stay in Kavala until somehow, by some miracle, the car was recovered. Marcus had a theory about how they were going to find somewhere to stay. You go to the nearest café, he said, and sit down and order drinks; after a while you become friendly with one of the waiters, who without doubt has a cousin who has a friend who knows someone who has a spotlessly clean fisherman's cottage where the spotlessly clean fisherman's wife will treat you like royalty. This was what he had always done with Theo, and it had never failed.

'It won't work,' Philip said to Eleanor with a kind of gloomy relish.

'It might,' Eleanor said, giving Marcus credit.

Arriving at Kavala, they fought their way off the boat like Christmas shoppers with five minutes to go before closing time. Marcus's tall, blond head led the way. They struggled down the quay and arrived at the nearest café. The little town was like a circus at the height of the season. Eleanor, to her intense disbelief, saw someone wearing a hat with the emblem 'Kiss Me Quick' on the crown. The fact that they found an empty table, filthy though it was, was a miracle. Surrounded by suitcases, they sat and waited.

Ten minutes later a harassed waiter came for their order. Marcus ordered retsina, Eleanor domestica, Philip ouzo. The waiter did not only not look friendly; he did not look as though he owned a relative in the world.

'Shouldn't we try the hotels?' Eleanor asked timidly.

'Of course not,' Marcus said. 'Do have a little patience, darling.'

Twenty minutes later Eleanor got up as unobtrusively as possible and went inside the café. 'We ordered,' she said in careful English, 'retsina, domestica and an ouzo.'

'You are German?' the waiter asked suspiciously.

'No. English.'

'I come immediately.'

Ten minutes later he came. Marcus spoke to him in what sounded like beautiful Greek. He glowered.

'Shouldn't we try the hotels?' Eleanor asked.

'Do stop fussing, darling. It's all perfectly all right.'

Philip buried his nose in his ouzo. Eleanor looked at the seafront. She had never been to Blackpool or Coney Island, but this, she knew, was what they were like. No spotlessly clean fisherman would come within twenty miles of the place. Marcus caught the waiter as he flew past and asked him a question which caused the waiter to stare at him as though he had made an obscene proposition. Perhaps he had. The waiter was not only scornful, but angry.

'Any good?' Philip asked innocently.

'It'll be all right,' Marcus said calmly.

'I think I'm just going to look around,' Eleanor said, and asked Philip, 'Do you want to come with me?'

'Okay,' Philip said.

They walked purposefully, pushing their way through the crowds. They tried seven hotels. Not one had so much as an attic.

'What now?' Eleanor asked.

'The Tourist Office. Do your rich tourist act. You know—talk posh. Like Grandmother Bennet.'

'Supposing he doesn't understand English?'

'Talk posh just the same.'

Mrs. Bennet came to her rescue. Eleanor raised her voice slightly and treated the bald, friendly tourist officer as though he were a senior assistant at Harrods whom she had known all her life. Amazingly, it worked. He made a long telephone call and then told them that there was one free chalet in a five-star hotel complex two miles down the coast. But they would have to hurry. If they weren't there in half an hour it would undoubtedly be gone.

'Taxi,' said Philip.

They drew up outside the café where Marcus was quietly drinking his second bottle of retsina. He was appalled by their plan. He said it was absurd and extravagant and that this was no way to get to know the real Greece.

'You won't come, then?' Eleanor asked.

'Darling, I wouldn't dream of it. I shall find myself a perfectly adequate room here. Besides, somebody had to do something about the car.'

'I know. But I feel awful leaving you here.'

'Oh come *on*,' Philip said.

'We'll come back for dinner—meet you here at seven.'

'You don't have to feel guilty about him,' Philip said in the taxi. 'He's perfectly happy, you know.'

'I don't think so. I think he's having a horrible time.'

'Well, he wanted to come, didn't he? I mean, we never said we'd look after *him*.'

'I suppose it was a mistake,' Eleanor said.

Philip said nothing.

For three days, while they waited for the infinite complexities of recovering the car from Limnos to sort themselves out, Eleanor and Philip stayed in their five-star chalet and lay on the hotel's private beach and swam in the hotel's private sea and might have been anywhere in the world. Greece had disappeared. Marcus had found himself a room over an ice-cream parlour which even he admitted was disgustingly dirty and dreadfully uncomfortable. On one day only he agreed to come over to the hotel, but it was not a success. He was pining for Theo, for Marcel, for people who talked his language and understood his feelings. Even his gaiety was dimmed, he was peevish and sullen. Eleanor felt helpless. She wanted the advice and assistance of someone who didn't exist—Graham. Between the two antagonistic young men she was bitterly alone. On the day the car miraculously appeared on the quay she felt as jubilant as a child let out of school.

'You're going to Salonika, I imagine,' Marcus said.

'Yes. Today.'

'Then I'll leave you there, if you don't mind. I'm sure it won't break your hearts.'

'Oh, *Marcus* . . .' Eleanor said.

'No. Really. I'll spend a couple of days in Athens and then get back to Paris. I've got masses of work to do and Marcel gets in a hopeless mess without me.'

She was arguing very feebly. 'But when you've come all this way . . .'

'Well,' he said, and gave one of his old, ravishing smiles, 'We all make mistakes, darling, don't we? I hope you adore all those jokey ruins.'

It was pouring with rain in Salonika. They dropped him outside the airport terminal. Standing in the rain, he kissed her hand through the open car window and gave Philip a kind of wave. He was radiant once more. Eleanor knew that however often she saw him again, she had said goodbye to him for ever.

'What's the opposite of missing someone?' Philip asked later, lengthily stretched out on his hotel bed.

'I don't know. Why?'

'Because whatever it is,' he said, 'that's what I feel. Shall we have a look at Greece now?'

In retrospect the next ten days were like a long dream which is only partly remembered. She would always remember sitting on a high, craggy rock in Meteora with the sunset shuddering above the fortress monasteries while Philip pondered about becoming a monk and they decided that there was much to be said for the religious life. She would remember the caves of Joannina where the stalactites take a hundred and twenty years to grow two inches and the gardens of fossils glowing and shining so far under the earth. She would remember the theatre at Dodona, where they were entirely alone, Philip a small, solitary spectator, sitting as though he were seeing visions. Leaving him, she sat under a small oak tree in the ruins and felt as though she were part of the earth. But when she suggested to Philip that it was a good place for a picnic he was horrified: oak trees, he said, are sacred.

She would remember Arta, and the long adventure of trying to buy butter, and the beach they found by mistake where Philip dived through enormous waves, and sleeping in the sun burning herself. It was here that she began to realise they were going home, every kilometre taking them back to that dangerous life that she had temporarily forgotten. In Delphi she let him go to the temple alone, but he came back disgusted by the crowds, fretted by a sense of blasphemy. She would always remember sitting under the great trees at the monastery of Ossias Loucas, staring out over the valley while Philip went on some investigation; again, in a dream, pretending that she was with Kilcannon, whose face she had almost entirely forgotten. She would remember sharing rooms with Philip and the way that he laughed in his sleep, as though his dreams had some rich humour that he did not find in life.

The rest, the driving, the hotels, the meals, even most of their conversations, slipped out of her memory. They were back in Athens. Philip, disgusted at last by Greek food, sent Cressida a cable: 'Arriving OA 259 15.05 Monday please order roast beef.' They went to Plaka for their last dinner, and although the meal was inedible Philip could see the floodlit Akropolis and there was a fair with a ferris wheel whirling round under the stars. They walked back to the hotel arm in arm, both conscious of another imminent parting.

Cressida was at the airport to meet them. Her face looked strained, almost haggard.

'I brought your car,' she said. 'I didn't know what to do, I couldn't reach you . . .'

'Why?' Eleanor asked sharply. 'What's happened?'

The crowds were pushing all round them.

'I can't tell you here,' Cressida said desperately.

'Yes. You can. What is it?'

'It's Grandmother Bennet. She had a . . . stroke yesterday.'

'Yes?'

'They took her to hospital. She . . . died this morning.'

21

To be, as they say, stunned with grief is merciful. Eleanor's grief at Mrs. Bennet's death was intense, lively and bitterly conscious. For years she had been growing away from the old lady, leaving to wander blindly in some foreign solitude of her own. Nevertheless the rock, the background, the home had always been there. She could always return to it. In the moments of her greatest confusion there had always been a voice which, even though it seldom made an appropriate or understanding comment, had been decisive and clear. Without Mrs. Bennet, and all she had stood for, the world was anarchic, lawless. It was not only the death of an old woman it was the end of a reign.

How much part love played in her grief she didn't know. Possibly very little, less than in Cressida's and Daphne's. It was the sense of loss that was unendurable. The mother is dead, long live the mother and she was not capable of taking over. The Bennet spirit, which had at the most been a thing of habit, had died with its originator. She found herself going through the motions, even occasionally using the familiar phrases, but it was a sham. She was hollow. By giving her too much, Mrs. Bennet had taken too much away.

The old lady's will was short and to the point. Eleanor was to have the house. Various pieces of furniture, all of them quite valuable antiques, went to the children. She had very little money, and she wanted this to be put in trust for her first great-grandchild. She wanted to be cremated with no religious service and no flowers. For some reason, Eleanor found this last request unendurably selfish. She wanted to bury Mrs. Bennet in roses, to dispose of her with some ceremony and grace. With a superstitious feeling of guilt she cut a dozen roses and put them on the coffin.

Philip refused to go to Portugal before the cremation, so Eleanor explained as well as she could in a cable to Graham, and arranged for him to go the following day. Marcus rang and asked her if she wanted him to come, but was obviously very reluctant, so she thanked him and said it wasn't necessary. The service lasted five minutes. All the women, whose loss was greatest, cried in painful silence. Philip clenched his hands in his pockets and would not look at the coffin in which his grandmother was lying. The curtains were slowly, modestly closed and Mrs. Bennet slid quietly into the incinerator. They filed out in silence and followed the empty hearse most of the way home.

The writer had grudgingly given Daphne two days off, and she was going to drive Philip to the airport and put him on the plane for Lisbon. Mrs. Strathearn, who had not come to the cremation but sent a letter of almost awestruck sympathy, was also making her preparations for Portugal, although she was not going for another fortnight. Jessica and Juniper were going to do voluntary work in a school for mentally handicapped children in Scotland, and Daphne was taking them as far as London. Hereward, out of respect for an image and an era that he had never known, had stayed away. Most of the letters of sympathy stayed unopened on the hall table. The house was wide open to the warm day, but none of them stayed indoors. They sat about the garden as though at any minute tea would arrive, and brisk comfort, and directions about how to continue. The old lady's bedroom, where Eleanor would sleep, was polished to an almost unnatural gloss, the bed so fresh and smooth that it looked as though it had never been slept in.

'What are you going to do about the garden?' Daphne asked.

'I don't know. Try to keep it going for a while.'

'But you can't afford Franco and Mrs. Rogers down here, as well as London.'

'No. I shall have to sell it.'

'Here?'

'Yes.'

Curiously, it was Philip who said, 'But we *can't* live without here!'

'We'll have to.'

'Unless you lived here?' Cressida asked.

'She couldn't be stuck in the country all by herself,' Daphne said. 'She'd go round the bend. What's happened about this money Dad's meant to be giving you?'

'I don't know. Nothing. He's gone off to Portugal without signing anything, anyway.'

None of them felt it was the day for rage against Graham, or for even thinking about Graham. In the evening Eleanor found Philip investigating his Chippendale desk.

'Do you like it?' she asked.

'Yes. How much d'you think it's worth?'

'I've no idea. Quite a lot, I should think.'

'I mean, it wouldn't go in my room in London, would it?'

'No,' she said reluctantly.

'Well . . . anyway . . . do you think you could find out how much it's worth?'

'If you want me to.'

'Thanks awfully.'

They were exceptionally kind to each other that night, behaving with a gentleness that Mrs. Bennet would barely have recognised. They knew that Cressida's grief was the most loving, and touched her head or her hand or her shoulder as they passed in order to try to give her something to take away the pain. She found their sympathy unbearable, but accepted it with as much grace as she could. Daphne, with Hereward to think of, was the least affected and cooked a brisk meal which only Philip, who had been deprived of his roast beef, ate. Jessica took Juniper for a long walk in the dark; she lay in the grass and looked at the night and wondered where her grandmother had gone to and decided that she was still here, all around her, underneath her body, within reach of her stretching fingers; Juniper, quivering, seemed to sense her presence. Only Jessica, who had escaped Mrs. Bennet's domination and grown up free and foreign, believed that her grandmother was still alive.

Daphne, Jessica and Philip left very early the next morning. When they had gone Eleanor and Cressida, in their dressing gowns, sat and drank coffee in the garden.

'I don't know what to do,' Eleanor said.

'No. I know what you mean.'

'Should I stay here or go back to London?'

'Why go back to London?'

'What will you do?'

'I'll stay here with you for a bit,' Cressida said.

'Have you heard from Tom? Does he want you to go back?' Cressida shrugged her shoulders, turning her head away.

'And what about Ellis? Do you see him at all now Gwen's home?' She heard a faint echo of Mrs. Bennet's voice in her questions.

'Occasionally. While you were away . . . he sometimes comes round when he's drunk.'

'Does Gwen know?'

'I don't think he's told her.'

'I'd like to see Ellis,' Eleanor said. 'I think he's the only person I would like to see.' She meant apart from Graham, who must not be thought about.

'He's very fond of you,' Cressida said. 'Especially when he's sober.'

. . . . .

It was during this time in the country, with Graham and Philip abroad and everyone except Cressida gone, that Eleanor began to be haunted by the future. Ever since she had walked through the streets after posting her letter to Kilcannon, an illness had been growing inside her, an apprehension that had now become an appalling fear. In Greece she had called it loneliness, and taken refuge in fantasies. Now, living in Mrs. Bennet's house with the knowledge that Cressida might leave her at any time, she could no longer deny the awful extent of her terror. She was alone, and it was unbearable. She did not know how to stop being alone. Mrs. Bennet's death had shattered her last few illusions that she could be solitary, independent and autonomous. What could she do about the future? How could she people it, furnish it, give it some life? There seemed no way. She felt absolutely powerless.

Cressida, seeing her mother looking so bleak and ill, thought she was mourning Mrs. Bennet. She suggested calling the doctor, a sensible man who had known them all for over twenty years. Finding Eleanor perfectly sound, he prescribed a dexadrene compound which gave her a certain external composure but did not touch the dreadful alarm in her heart. In spite of sleeping pills, she woke every morning at four or five and lay with her head buried in the pillow, trying to blot out the noise of her thoughts. The worst danger was the image of Graham. Asleep, she had no protection against her dreams; awake, she fought the image desperately, counting up to ten over and over again, trying to remember poems learned in her childhood, the chronology of kings, recipes, facts, anything to bar him from her mind. She knew that she should get up, do something, dig holes and fill them up again, scrub a clean floor, cook a meal that would never be eaten. Often she tried to grasp the problem, to reason with herself: life with Graham had been intolerably painful and humiliating, an impossibility. But this too was an impossibility: the days, weeks, months, years to come were a vast overhanging cliff which led in the end to death and which she had no hope of climbing. Why not just let go? This was the only solution that gave her some sense of peace and comfort. If only they would all understand, without grief or anger, that she could at last be merciful to herself, blaming no one, her love and hope for them all unshaken. Mrs. Bennet's voice seemed to come from beyond her own grave: wicked, cruel, unthinkable, unforgivable.

After Mrs. Bennet had stifled what Eleanor felt to be her only hope, she would be trapped into remembering again and again, 'We'll get married in October . . . We'll be together in the autumn.' But however much she wanted and needed to believe it, she knew this was the worst lie of all. Graham had found a perfectly pleasant way to live. She was no longer his concern. She was nobody's concern, except her children's, and they must all leave her in the end. She would not have it otherwise, and yet in her dreams they were always very young, dependent on her, creating terrible chaos. There were many people in her dreams, and sometimes Graham loved her. It was waking up to the truth that was unendurably painful.

Philip had a few days at home between coming back from Portugal and going to school. She met him at the airport and told him they were going back to Grandmother Bennet's, which seemed to please him. She thought he had grown even taller, and he was brown and cheerful. He did not notice how thin she had got, or how her voice shook. She did not ask many questions about Portugal, because she couldn't bear to hear about it, and he only told her that it had been smashing, a smashing house.

'Did you find out how much that desk is worth?'

'The man from the antique shop said about £200.'

'My God! Can I sell it, then?'

'It's yours. Of course you can sell it if you want to, though it seems a pity.'

'Two hundred pounds isn't a pity. Can we go and see him tomorrow?'

'Yes, if you like.'

She was terrified that he would notice how depressed and incompetent she had become. In an utterly foolish way she was even afraid that he would compare her with Nell Partwhistle and find her lacking. But he did not appear to notice anything and went whistling about the place as though genuinely happy to be back. The next morning they went to the antique shop in the local town and made a deal with Mr. Truscott. He said he would come up and fetch the desk in the afternoon, and who should he make the cheque out to?

'Philip Stanley Strathearn,' Philip said.

'You'll be sorry, young man, that you haven't kept that desk,' Mr. Truscott said.

'I don't think so,' Philip said.

'What will you do with the money?' Eleanor asked.

'Put it in the Post Office.'

He went off to do this while Eleanor tried to do some shopping. To go into the shops at all was an effort; to decide what to buy seemed almost impossible. She and Cressida had lived on eggs and cheese. The sight of steak was revolting; she bought at random everything that she could remember Philip liked. For the first time she was almost looking forward to him going back to school, so that she would no longer be exposed, or possibly found out.

On the day before he went back to school he was very busy, taking the bus into the town and shutting himself away for hours in his room. In the afternoon he took a letter to the post-box and when he came back was suddenly very affectionate to her, hugging her and saying, 'Hullo. How are you, then?'

The easy tears, released at any sign of kindness or love, were blotted against his hair. 'Fine,' she said, 'How are you, then?'

He showed great consideration for her all evening, insisting on pouring her a whisky and soda and lighting her cigarettes and making coffee for her after dinner. Cressida, sisterly, asked him if he was feeling quite well. When Eleanor said good night to him he suddenly clung to her like a child. They were both unable to hang on to each other for comfort and howl together. They cried secretly, pretending that it was not happening.

Cressida wanted to go up to London for the day, so took Philip in Eleanor's car. He would, he said quite firmly, find his own way to the station.

'Write,' Eleanor said, as always.

'I will,' he said, as always.

'And I'll come down and see you.'

'That'll be nice.'

'And then,' she said, with a feeling of total disbelief, 'it'll be Christmas.'

'Yes. Goodbye.'

'Goodbye, darling.'

She was alone. It was almost a relief to be able to fling herself on to the grass and weep without anybody watching, worrying. It occurred to her that she could lie here all day, sprawled like a corpse. What are we going to do about Nelly? Get up, child, pull yourself together, every cloud has a silver lining and it's always darkest before dawn. Oh, Mother, you don't understand. Nonsense, dear, I understand perfectly, a cup of strong tea and a couple of aspirin and you'll be right as rain. But I want . . . I want . . . Graham? There was no reply. Mrs. Bennet had always kept her own counsel about Graham. Mrs. Bennet was dead, dead, dead. Graham was dead, dead, dead. What dreadful cruelty kept her alive?

After nearly two hours she got up and went into the house. She approached Philip's room reluctantly, with dread, but at least clearing it up gave her something to do. She stripped the bed, tidied the table, put a couple of books back on the shelf. She picked up the wastepaper basket, intending to empty it, and saw that it was half full of screwed-up pieces of writing paper. Curious, she took out one of the balls of paper and smoothed it flat. It was a draft of a letter that had obviously been written many times, so many words were crossed out that at first she could hardly decipher it:

Dear Sir,

Regarding my joining your expedition to Northern Afghanistan in December, I am now sending you a money order for £169. I am seventeen years old and my parents are both dead so therefore I look after myself. Will you please let me know at the above address where I am to meet you on December 17th.

Yours faithfully,
Philip Stanley Strathearn

At first she smiled—of course it couldn't be serious. She read the letter again and her smile died. 'I am seventeen years old and my parents are both dead so therefore I look after myself.' It was deadly serious. Whether he went or not—and there was an icy knowledge that he would go—his intention was absolutely clear: he had grown up, he had left her, he was getting out. She sat down on the bed, the crumpled paper in her hand. 'Philip?' she asked; the answer was a door slammed in her face: 'Philip.'

22

Mrs. Strathearn came nimbly back from Portugal and suggested, almost before she had unpacked, that she come to stay for a few days. Cressida, who had grown very silent and abstracted, said that in that case she would go to London. Eleanor was not sure whether she felt capable of entertaining Mrs. Strathearn, but her longing to hear about Graham overcame her dread of hearing about him. The prospect of seeing his mother in fact gave her strength, as though she had found a bridge over some enormous abyss. She was still Mrs. Strathearn's daughter-in-law. It was a kind of identity, however obscure.

Mrs. Strathearn's motives were a little confused. She was very far from being malicious, and yet the idea of telling Eleanor about Graham and Nell Partwhistle moved her to a kind of glee. Eleanor must surely, after all these years, want nothing but Graham's happiness. She must surely realise that in middle age it was proper for women to take a back seat. Her own husband having died at an early age, she had never had to relinquish power, or adapt herself to the idea that she was no longer loved. She had no doubt that her dead husband, wherever he might be, was entirely faithful to her. If she suspected that Eleanor was, in her own terms, 'upset', she had little patience with it. Although without any moral sense in the Bennet meaning of the words, she had a strong sense of propriety and an almost touching belief in the conventions of her long-ago youth. Graham might be portly and balding: nevertheless it was perfectly acceptable that he should take a twenty-two-year-old mistress in preference to his wife. Eleanor might be slim and even, at times, beautiful: nevertheless she should buy a Siamese cat and take up bridge and make the best of it. These were the laws of nature, and for herself Mrs. Strathearn was quite satisfied with them. To resent them was what she termed making a fuss. Remembering certain incidents in the past, tears and slammed doors and dreadful silences, she fervently hoped that Eleanor was not going to make a fuss.

Eleanor didn't. She armoured herself in calm. She even found herself pleased to see the little elegant old lady with her neat nylon ankles and pretty shoes, her hands like wafers, her bluish hair neatly head-shaped, her matching luggage. Driving back from the station, she was able to listen quite pleasurably to the delights of Portugal, the magnificent view (Philip will have told you, of course), the swimming pool, the admirable servants. But she didn't want to hear any more. Mrs. Strathearn, looking brightly about her at the dying countryside, bided her time. She enquired about Marcus, Cressida, Daphne and Hereward, Jessica and Philip. She suggested that perhaps Philip might like her to take him to a matinée when he came home from school. Eleanor, thinking of Northern Afghanistan, said he might like that. When they reached the house Mrs. Strathearn suddenly put her lilac-gloved hand over Eleanor's:

'You must miss her dreadfully.'

'Yes,' Eleanor said.

'You know . . . Graham was very upset.'

'Was he,' Eleanor said.

They ignored the sudden chill of loss in Eleanor's heart, and went to look at the roses. Mrs. Strathearn's knowledge of roses came from her bedroom wallpaper. She thought they were pretty, in a damp and overblown way. She shivered rather elaborately and suggested that they went indoors, where she hoped she would be offered a dry sherry. Eleanor lit the fire and offered her a dry sherry. She herself had a large whisky. They settled down, Mrs. Strathearn in Mrs. Bennet's wing chair with her feet neatly crossed, Eleanor lying on the sofa. Although she looked relaxed and at ease, every muscle was tense, even her face was clenched. She knew that she was about to undergo a hardly bearable degree of torture.

They spoke of food, which had been excellent in the house but not so good in the restaurants. Eleanor saw them sitting in restaurants, Graham between Nell Partwhistle and his mother, a half-finished bottle of wine on the table (Graham would order another) and a litter of shellfish. There had been guests, two friends of Nell's (the first time her name was mentioned) and a couple called Radnage, though Mrs. Strathearn had the impression that they weren't married. The table grew to include two faceless girls chirruping together, and a ghost couple who did not know of the existence of Eleanor. Sometimes, Mrs. Strathearn said, They went out to dinner—she felt They didn't always want her with Them—and then she would stay at home and have an omelette cooked by Maria, and do her embroidery. Now the table shrank, was outside on a terrace somewhere, the sea down below, Graham was holding Nell Partwhistle's hand.

'More sherry?' Eleanor asked, moving suddenly off the sofa.

Mrs. Strathearn absently held out her glass.

'And often in the evenings we would play bridge. That was very nice. Do you know, Nell had never played bridge before?'

'Really,' Eleanor said.

'She picked it up remarkably quickly.'

'How clever of her,' Eleanor said.

There was a quick look, no more than a twitch of the

wrinkled eyelids, which said this remark was not worthy of her and was she going to make a fuss. Don't you see, Eleanor wanted to say or shout, I need you, a mother, his and therefore in some way mine, but don't tell me how happy he is because I can't bear it. She poured herself another whisky.

'And Graham . . .' she asked. 'Is he . . . happy?'

'Oh, very, I think,' Mrs. Strathearn answered promptly.

'And . . . the girl?'

'He seems devoted to her.'

It was too early to get the dinner. They were trapped. Perhaps Mrs. Strathearn was taken in by the apparently casual questions, the look of tolerant amusement that Eleanor had bolted and padlocked over her face.

'Of course, there's the question of age . . . A girl of that age, she ought to be out dancing, not sitting at home playing bridge.'

'I am sure,' Eleanor said, 'that Graham takes her out dancing.' Picture of Graham in his shirt-sleeves, sweating a great deal and pounding about the floor with a sort of pistoning movement, his mouth gaping. Did she love or hate this man?

'I think Nell would like to marry and have a baby,' Mrs. Strathearn said dreamily.

'Then why doesn't she?' Eleanor asked, with a complete conviction of insanity. Mrs. Strathearn came back to earth and looked at her with bland enquiry. 'Why don't I divorce him and let him . . . marry the girl?'

Oh dear, Mrs. Strathearn thought uneasily, is it a fuss? She put her glass down, brushed a non-existent crumb off her lap.

'Well,' she asked, 'I mean . . . how would you get a divorce?'

'In the usual way.'

'But desertion . . .'

'I'm not talking about desertion,' Eleanor said roughly, amazing herself. 'He left me to live with her. Adultery.'

The ugly, old-fashioned word lay between them like a challenge. Who was going to pick it up? Not Mrs. Strathearn.

She gazed down at the faded Persian rug, where it might be lying, and drew her feet in under her chair.

'Oh, I don't think . . .' she said; and then, still not looking at Eleanor, 'How could you, anyway?'

'Graham,' Eleanor found herself saying, 'is a household word.' She did not flinch at the absurd phrase. It sounded exactly right. 'Everybody knows about Graham.'

A flicker of something that might have been pleasure on the old lady's face—she was quite pleased that everybody knew about her son. She asked, without malice, 'But haven't you . . . ? I mean, there would be discretion statements and so on. Such a fuss.'

'There needn't be any fuss.' She was urging this divorce, which would undoubtedly kill her, as one might urge an executioner to get on with it. 'Not nowadays.'

'But to be divorced for adultery . . . wouldn't it be bad for his career? People might think . . .'

There were a number of answers to this: too bad, he should have thought of that before. But suddenly she knew that where Mrs. Strathearn and Graham were concerned there was no more question of justice than there would be between herself and Philip. She herself was sitting in the wing chair, and some faceless woman—a pleasant enough woman, no doubt, but a stranger—was delivering bitter judgement on Philip and she was unable to understand it. All that would matter would be that Philip continued to love her, his mother, and be faithful to her, his mother, and kind to her; and if he left his wife for some chit of a girl (she was possessed, at this moment, by Mrs. Bennet) she would honestly be glad, for there would be no serious competition any longer and she would be reinstated as comforter and provider, the female head of the family. Momentarily perched inside Mrs. Strathearn's head, she knew that she didn't want Graham (in other words, Philip) to be happily married. He could have all the Nell Partwhistles he liked, and treat them as abominably as he liked, and she would indulge the pretty creatures for his sake. But Eleanor would, in this situation, have no sympathy for Eleanor.

'I don't think I shall sell this house, after all,' she said. 'I would like to leave it to Philip.'

'But my dear . . .' Mrs. Strathearn, whose head had been quite unconscious of Eleanor's invasion, was nevertheless relieved to leave an upsetting subject, 'How can you manage two houses? Don't you need the money?'

'I don't see why I should sell this for money.' She was really being very dour, not at all charming. 'I think my mother did enough for us, really . . . I don't see why I should have to live on her now.'

'No, but . . . the London house was very expensive, wasn't it? Graham told me . . .'

'Yes,' she snapped. 'Houses in London are very expensive.'

Now something had to be done. Mrs. Strathearn was unhappy. Eleanor felt like an unattractive, sullen child demanding to be loved. She didn't want to reassure Mrs. Strathearn or look after her or cook her dinner or turn on her electric blanket for her. She wanted Mrs. Strathearn to do all these things for her, Eleanor, and to understand why she was raw and sour and so unlike the charming girl Graham had so disastrously married over a quarter of a century ago.

'I'll see to the dinner,' she said, and poured Mrs. Strathearn another glass of sherry.

For the rest of the evening Portugal was only mentioned in passing, that is the conversation hurried past it with no more than a sideways glance.

'Graham was so good,' Mrs. Strathearn said. 'He gave up his bedroom to me, with a private bath . . .'

'When Philip and I were in Greece,' Eleanor said, 'we sometimes had to share a room, and do you know . . . he laughs in his sleep?'

Mrs. Strathearn said that was odd, while Eleanor was turning Nell Partwhistle out of her (their) double bed, gathering up her bikinis, stowing them away in a secondary, twin-bedded room with a bathroom down some narrow, sunny corridor. Earlier in the day, before Mrs. Strathearn had arrived, she had indulged for a moment—chopping onions?—in a fantasy in which Mrs. Strathearn, blushing a little, had said, 'You know, it's most odd, but they don't . . . *sleep* together.' Who, then, she had wondered, would Nell Partwhistle sleep with? Of course, her fantasy had told her, it's ridiculous, they don't have any sex, or if they do it's so perverse (half a dozen girls, probably, all crawling around like puppies) that it hardly matters. She remembered the fantasy, and angrily called it a lie. She blamed Mrs. Strathearn for sleeping so beatifically in the borrowed bedroom, while only next door . . .

'But you *enjoyed* Greece,' Mrs. Strathearn was stating. 'And it was nice to see Marcus.'

'He's getting rather fat,' Eleanor said cruelly. 'Like Graham.'

'And there's no sign of him getting married?'

'Do you want to play Scrabble?' Eleanor asked hopelessly.

They played Scrabble, and Mrs. Strathearn put 'bugger', which she said, quite correctly, meant a Bulgarian heretic. She won, and was immensely pleased, finding that Eleanor looked quite attractive again and the sitting room pleasant and the prospect of the dead Mrs. Bennet's bed unalarming. She slept a little, with her eyes open, during the News. Immediately it was over she went to bed, self-sufficient, minding her own business, offering Eleanor a cheek like tissue to which her daughter-in-law gave a warm kiss which did not displace it.

Alone, Eleanor put more wood on the fire, poured herself another drink. She walked round the room as though inspecting it, but in reality trying to sort out, to sharpen her anguish into a kind of anger. It was useless. But finally the need to communicate with Graham was irresistible. She sat down and wrote him a letter which he would get on his return:

Dear Graham,

    I need to see you very much. I shall be in London by the time you get back. Will you ring me?

Love,
Eleanor

She put the note in an envelope, addressed and stamped it. When she had finished she sat very still, listening. Silence, emphasised rather than broken by the hissing of the logs, the drip of a tap in the kitchen, the infinitesimal creak and snap of the outside world, dazed her. She thought about Philip. She thought about tomorrow, and the day after, and next year. She thought about Mrs. Bennet, who was dead. What did she really want? Graham? Yes. Yes. I want all those years, all that enormous depriving love. Shall I ever tell him the truth? No, I am a liar by nature. In the autumn, in October, when we are old . . . She had to believe in lies. As she sat in Mrs. Bennet's wing chair, the fire dying, they were her only comfort.

23

But it had been bravado to say that she was going to leave the house to Philip. She couldn't afford to keep it, and Rothman, Rich and Bite agreed with her. A draft Deed of Separation trundled back and forth between London and Portugal. Graham objected to certain words and phrases, and in time Messrs. Crookston, Push and Mandeville expressed his objections to Messrs. Rothman, Bich and Bite. In the meanwhile Eleanor lived on the residue of the money Graham had given her to go to Greece. She put Mrs. Bennet's house in the hands of an estate agent and with sickening fear returned to London. After a few days the dead house began to come a little alive. It did not live, but it ticked over. She slept again in her off-white bedroom, remembering how in another life she had prepared it for Kilcannon. Cressida now slept next door, in what had been Jessica's room. There were no longer conferences around the kitchen table. Daphne was overworked between the writer and Hereward, and seldom came to see them. Jessica wrote scrawled letters from Scotland, where it seemed she was happy. Eleanor dared not think of Cressida returning to America, but she lived so much in the future, and in dread of the future, that when the news came she was hardly surprised.

'By the way,' Cressida said, 'I'm going back to Virginia on October 3rd.'

'Oh yes?' Eleanor said.

There was a long pause. Then Cressida said, 'And there's another thing.'

'What's that?'

'I'm pregnant.'

'You're *what*?' She had heard perfectly well.

'Pregnant.'

'Are you sure?'

'Absolutely.'

'Is it Ellis's?'

'Yes. It happened one night when you were away, when he came round after he'd had a row with Gwen. I knew it had happened, I don't know why.'

'Does he know?'

'No. And he mustn't. Please.'

'Why?'

'Because . . . he has Gwen. And I . . . have Tom.'

'But what are you going to tell Tom?'

'I don't know. I haven't decided. Anyway, I shall have it.'

'Oh, Cressie . . .' She took her eldest daughter's hand, but could not get any closer to her. 'What a mess.'

'It's not a mess! It's what I've always wanted, you know that! I thought you might be a bit . . . happy or encouraging or something! It's not much help to sit about saying what a mess.'

'I'm sorry. So that's why you've been so broody the past few weeks. Why didn't you tell me?'

'I wasn't sure till I'd had a test. And you seemed so low anyway . . .'

There was a pause. For both of them this could have been possibly could be, the best and most reviving thing that could happen. If Cressida stayed here and had the baby . . . it was like the world being suddenly flooded with light.

'Why are you going back to America?'

'Because I want to be with Tom.'

'But supposing when you tell him . . . he doesn't want you there?'

'I may not tell him, may I?'

'What d'you mean?'

'I may not tell him for a bit.'

'You don't mean . . . you'd try to let him think it was his?'

Cressida said nothing. She played with her coffee spoon, turning it over and over in her fingers.

'Cressida, you can't! You were always saying how you couldn't cheat him . . .'

'I'm not saying I'm going to! I'm just going to see, that's all . . . how he feels.'

She had obviously worked it out, in a confused sort of way. There was nothing to be done. The light had gone out again, leaving the world even darker than before. Eleanor, who had thought so often of the day and the hour when Cressida would leave, was actually living through what up till now had been a nightmare. She recognised everything that happened, all the preparations for departure, the shopping, the packing, the suitcases brought up from the basement. Her fear was physical; she shook with terror. It was no use trying to hide it from Cressida. The girl knew that her mother was ill, but stubbornly continued with her plan because there was nothing else to do, she must live her own life, she must go her own way, however painful. Eleanor knew this. If anyone had suggested to her that she should ask Cressida to stay, she would have violently refused. They kept slightly apart from each other, afraid of damaging each other by any closer contact.

At last the day, the moment, came. A hired car waited outside to take Cressida to the airport, the driver took all the suitcases from the hall.

'You'll . . . let me know what happens?'

'Of course I will. And take care of yourself.'

'If you stay . . . I might come over. When you have the baby.' A pin-point of light on a remote horizon.

'Yes. That would be lovely. Goodbye, then.'

'Goodbye.'

They kissed rather remotely, afraid of any explosions of grief. Eleanor closed the front door before Cressida had gone down the steps.

24

'I got your letter,' Graham said.

'Letter? Oh . . . yes.'

'When shall I come and see you, then?'

'I don't mind. It doesn't matter. Whenever you can.'

'Well . . . I'll come round for a drink on Saturday.'

'All right.'

'Have you heard from Philip?'

'No.'

'Are you all right?'

'Yes. I'll see you on Saturday.'

She had not spoken to anyone except the little Irish cleaner for three days. She did not go out. She got up in the morning and put on the same clothes that she had worn for days, brushed her hair and spent her days in her empty house. Once or twice she made herself write to Philip and Jessica, and gave the letters to the cleaner to post. She did not watch television, because it seemed an unbearable intrusion. She tried to read, but nothing made any sense. Daphne seemed to have disappeared, and she did not ring her up. She indulged in the fantasy of suicide as once she had indulged in fantasies of love. The idea of death was appallingly attractive and she played with it dangerously, letting it fill her mind to the exclusion of all reality. Mrs. Bennet never came near her now. She did not know that Ellis, and even Alex, kept meaning to ring her up. She did not know that Daphne, rushing back from work to cook Hereward's dinner, was worried about her. She lived with death, an evil and beautiful companion.

On Saturday, after catching sight of herself in the mirror, she washed her hair and put on a different sweater. The effort was appalling. Standing by the window waiting for Graham she had a vision of all the ordinary people in the world, working, hurrying about, talking to each other, catching buses and trains, shopping, eating, all consumed with some sort of purpose. Graham was like that. Probably Nell Partwhistle was like that. Could she recover by some strength of will; simply say to herself 'I will be better'? No. But why not? What was this mysterious terror that paralysed her? At one time, she thought, people used to die of broken hearts. That was the nearest she could get to understanding her condition: her heart was broken. She knew there were drugs you could take to deal with depression. But she was not depressed. She was dreadfully sad, and dreadfully frightened.

Graham arrived an hour late with a bottle of champagne. He was appalled by the way she looked, but said nothing in case she should tell him what was wrong. He looked brown and well.

'Who's here?' he asked.

'Nobody.'

'Cressida's gone back to America?'

'Yes.' She was not going to tell him that Cressida was pregnant, it would only make him angry. To be so close to him, and to know that he was going away, was insupportable. She must somehow live in the present, now, somehow confine herself to this brief hour.

'Well, what did you want to see me about?'

'I . . . Philip's made some plan to go away. To Northern Afghanistan. He's paid the money and everything. He sold the desk my mother left him.'

'Really?' He chuckled, lighting a cigar. 'That's very enterprising of him.'

'Perhaps you could talk to him about it?'

'Yes. Yes, of course. He was marvellous in Portugal.'

'Yes. He seemed to enjoy it.'

'How's everything else, then? You look,' he said reluctantly, 'a bit . . . washed out.'

I'm dying, Graham, I'm dying. Help me, please. She said, 'No, I'm not . . . very well.'

He said casually, 'I'd better come back to you, I suppose.'

'What do you mean?'

'Well, I could come back to you and have a string of girlfriends, like I did before.'

'Oh, *Graham* . . .' There was still a little unsuspected life in her. 'You know it wouldn't work. We'd both be miserable.'

'I wish you could make your own life. I mean, a proper life for yourself.'

'So do I.'

'It's no good for you, sitting alone in this great house. Why don't you have someone living in or something?'

'It's not a great house. I have to keep Philip's room, and a room for . . . Jessica or Cressida or whoever wants to come. That's all there is.'

'Oh, I wouldn't bother to do that. They can always find somewhere to stay.'

'But this is their . . . home.'

He gave up. 'Anyway, you know I love you.'

She stared at him and knew, for the first time, that their relationship was completely hopeless. It was as though she had never really seen him before. He was a stranger, whom she happened irrevocably to love; whom she would always love. But she must try her hardest never to see him again, never to think of him. She must pretend, as she had felt in the garden in the country, that he was dead. She must somehow confine her mourning to the natural mourning for someone who had died. The name of her present illness was Graham and it must, by some unknown method, possibly by a miracle, be cured.

'I have to go out,' she said.

'Oh. Well, then . . . I'll go.' They both stood up. He put his arms round her. 'Cheer up,' he said. 'Why don't you find a lovely lover or something?'

'Yes,' she said, her face against him. Goodbye, my darling; goodbye, my darling.

'It'll all come right in the end. When we're sixty we'll be together and sit in the sun somewhere and love each other till we die.'

'Yes,' she said.

'I'll talk to Philip, or write to him or something.'

'All right.'

'Goodbye, then. See you soon.'

'Goodbye, Graham.' Goodbye, Graham.

.   .   .   .   .

She took out the telephone directory and looked up Max Pepper. She did not believe he would be in on a Saturday evening, but in fact he answered the phone.

'This is Eleanor Strathearn. Do you remember, we met at the Brampton Arms?'

'Remember? I'll say I remember. I've been meaning to call you. What are you up to?'

'Well . . . I just wondered . . . whether you were free this evening?'

'Free? I certainly am. Why don't you come on over? We'll have a bite of dinner and a nice long chat.'

'I'll be there about eight.'

'Come as soon as you like. I'll be waiting.'

She gave herself a neat treble whisky and went upstairs to make herself desirable to Max Pepper.

25

If she had expected anything, his flat would have been what she had expected: huge lamps with silk shades, two great sofas opposite each other, an electric fire with firelit coals, some quite reasonable paintings, a bar with four high stools.

'This is great,' he said. 'It's great to see you again. You look wonderful.'

'Thank you.' She arranged herself on one of the sofas.

'What will you drink?'

'Scotch, please.'

'On the rocks, soda, water, what?'

'On the rocks would be fine.'

He fussed about behind the bar. He was as she remembered him, stout and red-faced; but there was a certain kindness and concern about him that made her smile, and arch her neck, and try to please him. When he had poured the drinks he sat next to her on the sofa.

'And how's the boy?'

'He's very well.'

'He's a great-looking boy. Looks a lot like you.'

'Really? Do you think so?'

'I think Russell's outgrowing the place. All he thinks about is girls.'

She made some kind of sound.

'Like father, like son, eh? I was an old man by the time I

was his age. Of course, I never had any real education. Still, I haven't done too badly without it, eh? I suppose one wants the best for one's kids . . .'

He talked on. Sometimes she nodded, sometimes she just smiled. I have said goodbye to my husband for ever and I am ill and what you see sitting here, smooth and elegant, is a dead body. 'Yes,' she said. 'Really? . . . Of course . . .', and laughed when his face showed her that she should laugh.

'I'm so glad you called tonight. Don't think I wasn't going to call you, but I've been very tied up, and I suppose you have a pretty busy life, eh?'

She smiled.

'I bet you do. There aren't many smart, available dames around. Mind you, I'm not saying you're available. Or are you?'

'I told you,' she kept smiling, 'I'm in no-man's-land.'

'That's right. I remember. How come you haven't moved out by now?'

She shrugged her shoulders and smiled a little more.

'Well, I must say I'm glad. I've got you all to myself for the evening, eh?'

'That's right.'

'We'll have another drink on that.'

By the time they had had another drink his arm was across her shoulders. He was beginning to sweat a little and his voice was getting louder. She told herself, I am out in the world, I am making contact. She told herself that she was unjustified in criticising this kindly man. All right, Graham, I'm making a life for myself. She pretended to be bold and skittish, and enchanted him.

'D'you want to go out to dinner? I've booked a table.'

She disappointed him. 'Yes, I'd love to.'

'One more for the road, then?'

'All right.'

Fortunately he had a uniformed driver who ushered them into the back seat of the Austin Princess. Its registration number, although she did not notice it, was MP 1. On the way to the restaurant he held her hand, which she found perfectly bearable. The amount she had drunk had dulled the pain, and she tried to make herself believe that the touch of palm to palm was comforting.

She knew, of course, that Max Pepper was not in the slightest degree interested in her as a person. Their only point of contact was their sons; otherwise they lived in different worlds. Throughout the long dinner, course after course which she hardly touched, he kept up an almost uninterrupted monologue about himself. She heard once more about his two marriages, his house in Spain and his flat in St. Moritz. She heard about his last girl-friend, a real little bitch who had left him for a no-good television director. She heard about his childhood, his parents, his first job as a shoe salesman in California. All this time she thought about people who were different from herself: foreigners, invulnerable and self-preserving. They had no patience with or understanding for illness, unless it could show itself in spots or physical growths and wounds. They were strong, and ruled the world; and it was no good telling them that they were basically lost and lonely, because they could not afford to believe it. Poor people. And yet who was she to feel sorry for them, forlorn and despairing as she was? Why should she feel sorry for Max Pepper, whose very noise seemed to be a longing to fill a void? Why did she, of all people, feel that she knew some secret which was hidden from them?

Over the brandy she suddenly knew what she wanted above all else: to be looked after. It was a very simple idea, and made her look at Max Pepper directly, enquiring into his bleary blue eyes. He understood this as an invitation, and clasped her hand. I want to be looked after, she was saying. I want to be told what to do, and when to do it. I want infinite support. I need support for my strength, not my weakness. I am not Mrs. Bennet. I am Eleanor Strathearn, someone who needs love like life. Max Pepper was saying something about going back to the flat for a last brandy. I was ugly and old, she thought, when I said goodbye to Graham. That is how he will always remember me. Max Pepper is inviting me to bed. Very well, she thought, I will go. I will show Graham that I am wanted. But Graham will not be there.

They went back in the Austin Princess. He kissed her, and she recoiled, feeling dreadfully sick and wondering whether she could ask the driver to stop so that she could retch into the gutter while Max Pepper turned away, disbelieving. The sickness passed, and they went up in the lift. Max kissed her again in the lift, and she did her best, touching the back of his cropped grey hair. She knew she was indulging in some kind of obscure revenge, but it didn't matter, nothing mattered if she was going to come within reach of love.

'You're so beautiful,' he said on the sofa, 'with your sexy, crooked face.'

She didn't have to say anything.

'Come on,' he persuaded. 'You want to be loved. Don't you want to be loved?'

'Yes,' she said truly.

'I want to love you and kiss you and taste you . . .'

Oh God, she said to herself, this is wrong. Nevertheless, she allowed herself to be led to the bedroom. Watch, Graham.

'Take off your tights,' he said, and took off his jacket.

Obediently, rebelliously, she took off her shoes and tights and lay on the bed like a sacrifice. He came at her like a dog. He guzzled her, his grey head devouring between her legs like a crazed terrier. She opened her eyes and saw the light. Her sight wandered round the room. She closed her eyes. It was a rough, nibbling, masticating eternity. Occasionally, out of some sort of misplaced pride, she made herself make appreciative noises. Why didn't she straighten her legs and kick him out of her life and time? God, she thought, knows. Is this love? Is this having a lovely lover? At last he stopped, and looked up at her, smiling.

'Was that nice? Did you enjoy it?'

'Yes,' she lied, fooling him.

'You taste like you look. Beautiful and sexy and mad.'

She looked at Max Pepper and she thought, If this is love, if this is all there is, I'd be better dead. She sat up, reached for her tights and carefully pulled them on.

'You're happy?' Max Pepper asked anxiously. 'It was all right?'

'Of course,' she said.

'Good. Good.'

She stood up, fully clothed. 'I must go home now.'

'Robbins will drive you.'

'It's all right. I have my own car.'

'I'm crazy about independent women. You really have it all sewn up, don't you? Don't rely on anyone. I like that.' He kissed her warily and put on his jacket. 'When shall I see you again?'

'I'm going away,' she said. It was not really a lie. Perhaps she was going away for ever.

'Well, call me when you get back, eh?'

He took her down in the lift and saw her to her car. If he had made love to her with his stout, strong body she might even have felt comforted. She might even have had an affair with Max Pepper, content to think about something else while he talked, grateful at least for his kindness and appreciation. As it was she felt that fate, whatever fate was, had struck her a knock-out blow. Now, fate said, will you get it into your head that all your efforts are hopeless, that you are doomed.

'See you soon,' Max Pepper said. 'Don't forget.'

'I won't,' she said truthfully.

She drove home. The abandoned house, which only six months ago she had thought about with such hope, did not even contain any ghosts: Philip, Cressida, Daphne and Jessica had all left it. The furniture stood about unused. It was a great warehouse in which one woman lived alone, frightened out of her wits.

She had to hear herself speak, to hear a voice from the outside; otherwise she genuinely felt she would go mad. She telephoned the Answering Service.

'Sir Patrick Kilcannon called yesterday and said he would call again this morning.'

'Thank you.'

He hadn't called this morning. Anyway, when you tried to remember, who was Patrick Kilcannon? A small man on a gold chair. Would he feed her, warm her, offer her the loan of his bed? Never. He was two words of a long-forgotten song.

She did not dare to go upstairs, but at last slept where she was, by the telephone.

26

The next morning she had a letter from Cressida. Tom Mc-
Graw had seemed extremely glad to see her. He actually said
he had missed her. She had told him about the baby, after all.
He had actually seemed pleased, followed by four exclamation marks. He appeared to believe, strange man, that she had
taken some initiative, three exclamation marks. And he had
said that since it looked as though she was going to stay anyway, they might as well let people think that it was his baby.
Cressida was not so sure about this. She seemed to have
changed a lot, she said. She didn't think the same way about
things. Maybe she would just have her own baby, and leave
it at that. Anyway, life seemed very good to her one way and
another. She hoped it would soon be as good for Eleanor, to
whom she sent very much love.

That's good, Eleanor told herself. That's hopeful. She felt
a flicker of courage so small that it was hardly palpable. It
was not Mrs. Bennet's courage, of keeping a stiff upper lip
until pain inevitably passed. Such as it was, it was her own.
She thought of all the lies she had told people, Graham, her
children; pretending to be someone quite different from the
person she really was. She thought of all the deceits she had
practised by assuming that she must be strong and competent,
the queen of a miniature country. She was no queen. She
needed to be looked after and to be loved. And to serve? No,
that was part of the deceit. She had done enough serving in

her life. But to give? Yes, certainly. She had huge gifts in herself, and no one to give them to, nowhere to put them. The courage flickered, and seemed to go out. Yet she knew, as she climbed the stairs to bath and change out of her Max Pepper clothes (another deceit, which made her hate herself more than she could afford) that it would come back. Somehow, by some sort of trial and error, Eleanor Strathearn might at last be born. She noticed a patch of damp on the wall, and all the bleached puddles where Juniper had peed on her expensive carpet. I hate this house, she thought, and all it stands for. She was not strong enough yet for such rebellion. It shocked her. I must love this house because it is our home. Such care I took with this sunny house full of colour. But I must tell the truth, something in her insisted: I must learn to recognise it.

Nevertheless she wrote to Philip and Jessica, cheating, lying letters, making out that she was living a perfectly normal life, whatever that was. There was a pile of old newspapers, all unread, on the kitchen table. When she had stamped the letters she made herself open the top newspaper so that she would not, for a few moments at least, be exposed to the lurking terror. Life, she saw with amazement, was still being lived, or ended. There were still wars, aeroplanes were still crashing, children getting drowned in rivers, people were dying and getting born, being married and divorced. What was their secret? How could they stand it? Behind almost every item of news there was pain. Why were they all suffering alone? Was everyone in the world, apart from Graham and Nell Partwhistle, suffering? Why couldn't they all meet, and be together, and hold each other for comfort? Her eyes, which had been drifting across the pages, were suddenly held by a name:

'Actress Melanie Rose has been named in a divorce action brought against Sir Patrick Kilcannon by his wife, Lady Veronica Kilcannon.

'Miss Rose, twenty-eight, a Deb of the Year in the 1960's,

222

is living apart from her husband, actor Richard Wright.

'Films Miss Rose has appeared in include . . .'

She stopped reading for a moment. A brief, terrible hilarity broke loose in her. She covered her face with her hands and drew them slowly down until her eyes were exposed, but her mouth still hidden.

'. . . The Kilcannons married twenty-three years ago and have one daughter.

'The petition appears in the latest list of undefended actions for hearing in the London divorce courts.'

So this had been his trouble, his worry that he didn't want to bother her with. Her Gaelic knight. Poor man. He had been trying, when he needed it, to get in touch with her for comfort. Undoubtedly he would have told her all about it and might even have leant a little on her shoulder: her strong, feminine, maternal, always accessible shoulder. 'My God!' she said out loud, and looked for anger. There was none. Only pity and understanding and dreadful self-ridicule. First and always first, Graham; then Ellis and Alex and perhaps two or three others; then the fantasy of Kilcannon; lastly, the awful reality of Max Pepper. She had always lied to herself about men, because she had always thought she needed them so desperately. Well, she did. But she also needed the truth, and an end to games. She seriously needed to save her life.

She drove down to Wimpole Street and parked behind the Porsche, which was full of parcels. The receptionist was surprised to see her after so long.

'. . . I know Dr. Strathearn is dreadfully busy. He has two patients waiting for him now.'

'Please tell him I'm here.'

She went and sat in the waiting room, with its old copies of *Country Life* that reminded her of Philip. An actress patient of Graham's, wearing an inordinate amount of perfume and laced white boots, cooed at her: 'Don't tell me *you* have to join the queue now!'

Eleanor smiled briefly.

'How's the new house?' the actress asked.

'Fine,' Eleanor said. You see? It's impossible to tell the truth.

'Mrs. Strathearn,' the receptionist said.

She was taken up in the lift, not speaking. She was let in by a new secretary, a very pretty girl who seemed pleased to see her: liar.

'Go straight in, Mrs. Strathearn, please.'

He was standing by the window tapping something on his hand. He turned and asked, 'What do you want to come here for? I'm appallingly busy.'

She sat down in the black leather armchair. 'I had to see you. I . . . have something to say to you. I've never said it before.'

'Well?'

She asked, as though in her own home, 'Won't you sit down?'

He sat behind the desk. She lit her own cigarette.

'Well?' he asked again.

She said in a dead, strained voice, beyond tears, 'I'm rather . . . ill. That was why I asked you to come and see me the other day. But I didn't tell you the reason. I . . . pretended. Like I always have.'

'And what is the reason?' It suddenly occurred to her that he was dreading cancer, or some dreadful disease that he would have to pay attention to.

'I'm inconsolable,' she said practically, as though it were a word she frequently used. 'About us. About the situation.'

'Oh . . .' He swivelled, seemed about to get up, then lay back. 'I'm sorry. You mustn't feel like that.'

'But I do.'

'I don't . . . see what can be done about it.'

'No. I don't suppose there is anything to be done about it. I . . . just wanted you to know. I mean, there are two of us. You should know.'

224

'Oh, yes,' he said vaguely. 'You'll be all right in time.'

'Is Nell Partwhistle . . . permanent?'

'Nothing's permanent. But some sort of Nell Partwhistle —yes.'

'Why?'

'Because that's what I need.'

'Shall we get a divorce?'

'What on earth for? I don't want a divorce.'

'I see.' She got up. There was nothing to stay for. 'Well, then . . . goodbye.'

He heaved himself up and came over to her. She was wearing flat shoes and hardly reached up to his shoulder. He kissed her lovingly.

'Blessings on your tiny head,' he said. 'You know I'm very fond of you.'

And we'll get married, we'll be together in the autumn, we'll sit through our old age in the sun? She had already said goodbye to him once, but that too had been a lie. Now she knew the truth and must live with it. Must, must? What was this continual must?

Must meant the necessity of going down in the lift and smiling at the receptionist and going out into the street and getting into her car and driving home.

.   .   .   .   .

That evening she was lying in the sitting room with the curtains drawn back. It was already dark, and beginning to get cold. She had received a letter by the second post from the estate agent saying that there was a firm offer for Mrs. Bennet's house. The letter lay on the open newspaper on the kitchen table. She was remotely conscious of wanting a drink, but there was no drink in the house because she hadn't ordered any. No drink and no food. What a ridiculous situation, whispered some echo. What did people do who wanted food and drink? They went out and got it. Or somebody got it for them. Graham had always been very good at that. Toasted cheese and a glass of wine. Graham was dead. Her mother, all mothers, were dead. Out there, beyond the dark glass where she had sat for so long waiting for Kilcannon, wasn't there anyone or anything that would make her believe it?

She got up and went down the dark stairs, pulling her jacket off the hook and putting her purse in its pocket, but not taking her handbag. She saw her keys lying on the hall table. She looked at them for a moment with a kind of interest. Philip, Jessica, Daphne, Cressida all had keys to this house. She didn't need hers. She left them where they were and turned out all the lights. The slam of the front door seemed to resound down the street. Did she have neighbours? She didn't know. She walked across the street to the pub where she had been with Marcus.

It was full of people. It must be late, then. She pushed her way to the bar and at last ordered a whisky and soda. The girl in the PVC raincoat was there, sitting on her usual stool, alone. Bewildered by the noise around her, the huge faces with opening and shutting mouths, Eleanor backed against the wall.

'You on your own, then?'

She looked up and saw the girl: a kindly, rather plain face, with bedraggled hair.

'Yes.'

'Where's the young fellow you were with?'

'He's . . . gone.'

'Come and sit by me, then, if you're on your own.'

She followed the PVC raincoat, the girl found another stool from somewhere and they sat together.

'I've often seen you about,' said the girl. 'You live in that big house, don't you, over the road? Got a bit of a sporty car?'

'Yes,' Eleanor said.

'Live there all on your own, do you?'

'Yes,' Eleanor said. She noticed the girl's stubby hands, with a ring in the shape of a seahorse on her fourth finger.

'You shouldn't live on your own. People shouldn't be by themselves. It's not natural.'

'No,' Eleanor said.

'There's something the matter with you, isn't there? I was watching you. I can tell.'

'Yes,' Eleanor said.

'What is it, a man or a woman?'

'I don't know,' Eleanor said.

'Well, it's always you in the end, isn't it? I mean, especially when you're living on your own. You know what I think? I think you need a bit of looking after.'

'Yes,' Eleanor said.

'Got kids, have you?'

'Yes.'

'Well, they grow up, don't they. Is that scotch?'

'No, let me . . .'

'Pay day today. I work in a garage. Petrol pumps. Bloody boring, but the pay's not bad. Husband left you?'

'Yes,' Eleanor said. 'Well. We left each other.'

'Men,' the girl said, as though it were an expletive. She ordered two more drinks. Out of the corners of her slit brown eyes she was watching Eleanor carefully. 'Tell you what, why don't you come home with me and have a nosh? I've got some liver and bacon. Fancy liver and bacon?'

'I . . .'

'I wouldn't ask you if I wasn't a good cook,' the girl said. 'But I'm a good cook. I enjoy cooking. Mashed potatoes?'

'All right,' Eleanor said.

'You need something,' the girl said quietly.

'Yes,' Eleanor said.

'You can stay, if you like. There's plenty of room. My girl-friend's just moved out. You'd be comfortable, and I'd always be there . . . you know, if you felt lonely.'

'Thank you,' Eleanor said.

'Let's go, then, shall we? It's only just down the road. Good night, Harry,' she called, jaunty.

They walked on the opposite side of the road to Eleanor's home. She did not look at it. The girl put her arm through Eleanor's and helped her along.

27

THIS DEED OF SEPARATION is made the   day of   One Thousand Nine Hundred and Seventy One BETWEEN GRAHAM STANLEY STRATHEARN of 9 Russington Avenue, London E.11, Medical Practitioner (hereinafter called 'the husband') of the one part and ELEANOR STRATHEARN of 95 Graves Avenue, N.W.8. (hereinafter called 'the wife') of the other part

    WHEREAS the husband and the wife are living separate and apart from each other and agree to enter into the agreement hereinafter contained

    NOW THIS DEED WITNESSETH and it is hereby mutually agreed and declared by and between the parties hereto as follows

1. THE husband and the wife may live separate and apart from each other as if they were unmarried and shall each be free of the marital control of the other

2. (a) From and after the date hereof and until the happening of the first to occur of the events specified in sub-clause (b) of this Clause the husband shall pay or cause to be paid to the wife on the first day of every month such a balance of a sum of Two hundred and ninety-two pounds (£292) as remains after deducting income tax at the standard rate for the time being in force the first of

such payments to be made in advance on the first day of August 1971

(b) The events referred to in sub-clause (a) of this Clause are the following events namely

(i) the death of the husband

(ii) the death of the wife

(iii) the making of an order by the court whereby the husband is ordered to pay or secure to the wife or any other person any sum whether a lump sum or a periodical sum for the maintenance of the wife or to execute any deed or other document to provide for such maintenance

(iv) if the husband and the wife shall at any future time resume cohabitation or if their marriage shall by order or decree of a competent court recognised by the High Court in England be dissolved or annulled or if they be judicially separated

3. SUBJECT to the terms of Clause 4 hereof and until the happening of the first to occur of the events specified in clause (b) or Clause 2 hereof the wife shall out of the provision made for her by these presents and out of her separate estate or otherwise in all respects support and maintain herself and

(a) pay and discharge all the debts, engagements and liabilities which she may incur or enter into

(b) pay the cost of maintaining Philip Stanley Strathearn until he is of age except the cost of his education

(c) shall indemnify the husband his heirs executors and administrators therefrom and all actions proceedings costs damages expenses claims demands and liabilities on account thereof

4. FROM and after the date hereof and until the happening of the first to occur of the events specified in sub-clause (b) of Clause 2 the husband shall

(a) permit the wife to reside in the house known as 95 Graves Avenue aforesaid and shall pay all insurance, repairs, rates and water rates in respect of the said house so long as the wife shall continue to reside there-in

(b) not to sell the said house known as 95 Graves Avenue or dispose of any interest in the same without the prior written consent of the wife

(c) pay the cost of educating Philip Stanley Strathearn but shall permit the wife to exercise care and control of him while the husband retains custody

IN WITNESS whereof the hands and seals of the husband and the wife hereto set the day and year first above written

SIGNED SEALED AND
DELIVERED by the said
GRAHAM STRATHEARN
in the presence of :

Eleanor Partwhistle

SIGNED SEALED AND
DELIVERED by the said
ELEANOR STRATHEARN
in the presence of :

Eleanor Strathearn

Ellis Cromer